Arts and Crafts Exhibition Society, R. Clark, Ltd.

Arts and Crafts Essays

Arts and Crafts Exhibition Society, R. Clark, Ltd.

Arts and Crafts Essays

ISBN/EAN: 9783337367473

Printed in Europe, USA, Canada, Australia, Japan

Cover: Foto ©Andreas Hilbeck / pixelio.de

More available books at **www.hansebooks.com**

Arts and Crafts Essays

By

Members of the Arts and Crafts
Exhibition Society

With a Preface

By William Morris

London

RIVINGTON, PERCIVAL, & CO.

1893

PREFACE

THE papers that follow this need no explanation, since they are directed towards special sides of the Arts and Crafts. Mr. Crane has put forward the aims of the Arts and Crafts Exhibition Society *as* an Exhibition Society, therefore I need not enlarge upon that phase of this book. But I will write a few words on the way in which it seems to me we ought to face the present position of that revival in decorative art of which our Society is one of the tokens.

And, in the first place, the very fact

that there is a "revival" shows that the arts aforesaid have been sick unto death. In all such changes the first of the new does not appear till there is little or no life left in the old, and yet the old, even when it is all but dead, goes on living in corruption, and refuses to get itself put quietly out of the way and decently buried. So that while the revival advances and does some good work, the period of corruption goes on from worse to worse, till it arrives at the point when it can no longer be borne, and disappears. To give a concrete example: in these last days there are many buildings erected which (in spite of our eclecticism, our lack of a traditional style) are at least well designed and give pleasure to the eye; nevertheless, so hopelessly hideous and vulgar is general building that persons of taste find themselves regretting the brown brick box with its feeble and trumpery attempts at ornament, which characterises the style of building current at the end of the last and beginning of this century, because there is some style about it, and even some merit of design, if only negative.

The position which we have to face then is this: the lack of beauty in modern life (of decoration in the best sense of the word), which in the earlier part of the century was unnoticed, is now recognised by a part of the public as an evil to be remedied if possible; but by far the larger part of civilised mankind does not feel that lack in the least, so that no general sense of beauty is extant which would *force* us into the creation of a feeling for art which in its turn would *force* us into taking up the dropped links of tradition, and once more producing genuine organic art. Such art as we have is not the work of the mass of

Preface. craftsmen unconscious of any definite style, but producing beauty instinctively; conscious rather of the desire to turn out a creditable piece of work than of any aim towards positive beauty. That is the essential motive power towards art in past ages; but our art is the work of a small minority composed of educated persons, fully conscious of their aim of producing beauty, and distinguished from the great body of workmen by the possession of that aim.

I do not, indeed, ignore the fact that there is a school of artists belonging to this decade who set forth that beauty is not an essential part of art; which they consider rather as an instrument for the statement of fact, or an exhibition of the artist's intellectual observation and skill of hand. Such a school would seem at first sight to have an interest of its own as a genuine traditional development of the art of the eighteenth century, which, like all intellectual movements in that century, was negative and destructive; and this all the more as the above-mentioned school is connected with science rather than art. But on looking closer into the matter it will be seen that this school cannot claim any special interest on the score of tradition. For the eighteenth century art was quite unconscious of its tendency towards ugliness and nullity, whereas the modern "Impressionists" loudly proclaim their enmity to beauty, and are no more unconscious of their aim than the artists of the revival are of their longing to link themselves to the traditional art of the past.

Here we have then, on the one hand, a school which is pushing rather than drifting into the domain of the empirical science of to-day, and another which can only work through its observation of an art which was once organic, but which died centuries ago, leaving us what by this time has become but the wreckage of its brilliant and eager life, while at the same time the great mass of civilisation lives on content to forgo art almost altogether. Nevertheless the artists of both the schools spoken of are undoubtedly honest and eager in pursuit of art under the conditions of modern civilisation; that is to say, that they have this much in common with the schools of tradition, that they do what they are impelled to do, and that the public would be quite wrong in supposing them to be swayed by mere affectation.

Now it seems to me that this impulse in men of certain minds and moods towards certain forms of art, this genuine eclecticism, is all that we can expect under modern civilisation; that we can expect no *general* impulse towards the fine arts till civilisation has been transformed into some other condition of life, the details of which we cannot foresee. Let us then make the best of it, and admit that those who practise art must nowadays be conscious of that practice; conscious I mean that they are either adding a certain amount of artistic beauty and interest to a piece of goods which would, if produced in the ordinary way, have no beauty or artistic interest, or that they are producing something which has no other reason for existence than its beauty and artistic interest. But having made the admission let us accept the consequences of it, and understand that it is our business as artists, since we desire to produce works of art, to supply the lack of tradition by diligently cultivating in ourselves the sense of beauty (*pace* the Impressionists), skill of hand, and niceness of observation, without which only a *makeshift* of art can be got; and also, so far as we can, to call the attention of the public to the fact that there are a few persons who are doing this, and even earning a livelihood by so doing, and that therefore, in spite of the destructive tradition of our immediate past, in spite of the great revolution in the production of wares, which this century only has seen on the road to completion, and which on the face of it, and perhaps essentially, is hostile to art, in spite of all difficulties which the evolution of the later days of society has thrown in the way of that side of human pleasure which is called art, there is still a minority with a good deal of life in it which is not content with what is called utilitarianism, which, being interpreted, means the reckless waste of life in the pursuit of the means of life.

It is this conscious cultivation of art and the attempt to interest the public in it which the Arts and Crafts Exhibition Society has set itself to help, by calling special attention to that really most important side of art, the decoration of utilities by furnishing them with genuine artistic finish in place of trade finish.

WILLIAM MORRIS.

July 1893.

CONTENTS

PAGE

OF THE REVIVAL OF DESIGN AND HANDICRAFT: WITH NOTES ON THE WORK OF THE ARTS AND CRAFTS EXHIBITION SOCIETY

THE decorative artist and the handicraftsman have hitherto had but little opportunity of displaying their work in the public eye, or rather of appealing to it upon strictly artistic grounds in the same sense as the pictorial artist; and it is a somewhat singular state of things that at a time when the Arts are perhaps more looked after, and certainly more talked about, than they have ever been before, and the beautifying of houses, to those to whom it is possible, has become in some cases almost a religion, so little is known of the actual designer and maker (as distinct from the proprietary manufacturer or middleman) of those familiar things which contribute so much to the comfort and refinement of life—of our chairs and cabinets, our chintzes and wall-papers, our lamps and pitchers—the Lares and Penates of our households, which with the touch of time and association often come to be regarded with so peculiar an affection.

Nor is this condition of affairs in regard to applied Art without an explanation, since it is undeniable that under the modern industrial system that personal element, which is so important in all forms of Art, has been thrust farther and farther into the background, until the production of what are called ornamental objects, and the supply of ornamental additions generally, instead of growing out of organic necessities, have become, under a misapplication of machinery, driven by the keen competition of trade, purely commercial affairs—questions of the supply and demand of the market artificially stimulated and controlled by the arts of the advertiser and the salesman bidding against each other for the favour of a capricious and passing fashion, which too often takes the place of a real love of Art in our days.

Of late years, however, a kind of revival has been going on, as a protest against the conviction that, with all our modern mechanical achievements, comforts, and luxuries, life is growing "uglier every day," as Mr. Morris puts it. Even our painters are driven to rely rather on the accidental beauty which, like a struggling ray through a London fog, sometimes illumes and transfigures the sordid commonplace of everyday life. We cannot, however, live on sensational effects without impairing our sense of form and balance—of beauty, in short. We cannot concentrate our attention on pictorial and graphic art, and come to regard it as the one form worth pursuing, without losing our sense of construction and power of adaptation in design to all kinds of very different materials and purposes—that sense of relation—that architectonic sense which built up the great monuments of the past.

The true root and basis of all Art lies in the handicrafts. If there is no room or chance of recognition for really artistic power and feeling in design and craftsmanship—if Art is not recognised in the humblest object and material, and felt to be as valuable in its own way as the more highly rewarded pictorial skill —the arts cannot be in a sound condition; and if artists cease to be found among the crafts there is great danger that they will vanish from the arts also, and become manufacturers and salesmen instead.

It was with the object of giving some visible expression to these views that the Exhibitions of the Arts and Crafts Society were organised.

As was to be expected, many difficulties had to be encountered. In the endeavour to assign due credit to the responsible designer and workman, it was found sometimes difficult to do so amid the very numerous artificers (in some cases) who under our industrial conditions contribute to the production of a work.

It will readily be understood that the

organisation of exhibitions of this character, and with such objects as have been stated, is a far less simple matter than an ordinary picture exhibition. Instead of having an array of artists whose names and addresses are in every catalogue, our constituency, as it were, outside the personal knowledge of the Committee, had to be discovered. Under the designation of So-and-so and Co. many a skilful designer and craftsman may be concealed; and individual and independent artists in design and handicraft are as yet few and far between.

However, in the belief, as elsewhere expressed, that it is little good nourishing the tree at the head if it is dying at the root, and that, living or dying, the desirability of an accurate diagnosis while there is any doubt of our artistic health will at once be admitted, the

Society determined to try the experiment and so opened their first Exhibition.

The reception given to it having so far justified our plea for the due recognition of the arts and crafts of design, and our belief in their fundamental importance—the amount of public interest and support accorded to the Exhibition having, in fact, far exceeded our anticipations, it was determined to hold a second on the same lines, and to endeavour to carry out, with more completeness than was at first found possible, those principles of work, ideas, and aims in art for which we contended, and to make the Exhibition a rallying point, as it were, for all sympathetic workers.

Regarding design as a species of language capable of very varied expression through the medium of different methods and materials, it naturally follows that there is all the difference in the world between one treatment and another, both of design and material; and, moreover, every material has its own proper capacity and appropriate range of expression, so that it becomes the business of the sympathetic workman to discover this and give it due expansion.

For the absence of this discriminating sense no amount of mechanical smoothness or imitative skill can compensate; and it is obvious that any attempt to imitate or render the qualities peculiar to one material in another leads the workman on a false track.

Now, we have only to consider how much of the work commonly produced, which comes under the head of what is called "industrial art," depends upon this very false quality of imitation (whether as to design or material) to show how far we have departed in the

Of the Revival of Design and Handicraft.

ordinary processes of manufacture and standards of trade from primitive and true artistic instincts. The demand, artificially stimulated, is less for thought or beauty than for novelty, and all sorts of mechanical invention are applied, chiefly with the view of increasing the rate of production and diminishing its cost, regardless of the fact that anything in the nature of bad or false art is dear at any price.

Plain materials and surfaces are infinitely preferable to inorganic and inappropriate ornament; yet there is not the simplest article of common use made by the hand of man that is not capable of receiving some touch of art—whether it lies in the planning and proportions, or in the final decorative adornment; whether in the work of the smith, the carpenter, the carver, the weaver, or the potter, and the other indispensable crafts.

Of the Revival of Design and Handicraft.

With the organisation of industry on the grand scale, and the enormous application of machinery in the interests of competitive production for profit, when both art and industry are forced to make their appeal to the unreal and impersonal *average*, rather than to the real and personal *you* and *me*, it is not wonderful that beauty should have become divorced from use, and that attempts to concede its demands, and the desire for it, should too often mean the ill-considered bedizenment of meaningless and unrelated ornament.

The very producer, the designer, and craftsman, too, has been lost sight of, and his personality submerged in that of a business firm, so that we have reached the *reductio ad absurdum* of an impersonal artist or craftsman trying to produce things of beauty for an impersonal and unknown public—a purely conjectural matter from first to last.

Of the Revival of Design and Handicraft.

Under such conditions it is hardly surprising that the arts of design should have declined, and that the idea of art should have become limited to pictorial work (where, at least, the artist may be known, in some relation to his public, and comparatively free).

Partly as a protest against this state of things, and partly to concentrate the awakened feeling for beauty in the accessories of life, the Arts and Crafts Exhibition Society commenced their work.

The movement, however, towards a revival of design and handicraft, the effort to unite—or rather to re-unite—the artist and the craftsman, so sundered by the industrial conditions of our century, has been growing and gathering force for some time past. It reflects in art the intellectual movement of inquiry into fundamental principles and necessities, and is a practical expression of the philosophy of the conditioned. It is true it has many different sides and manifestations, and is under many different influences and impelled by different aims. With some the question is closely connected with the commercial prosperity of England, and her prowess in the competitive race for wealth; with others it is enough if the social well-being and happiness of her people is advanced, and that the touch of art should lighten the toil of joyless lives. The movement, indeed, represents in some sense a revolt against the hard mechanical conventional life and its insensibility to beauty (quite another thing to ornament). It is a protest against that so-called industrial progress which produces shoddy wares, the cheapness of which is paid for by the lives of their producers and the degradation of their users. It is a protest against the turning of men into machines, against artificial distinctions in art, and against making the immediate market value, or possibility of profit, the chief test of artistic merit. It also advances the claim of all and each to the common possession of beauty in things common and familiar, and would awaken the sense of this beauty, deadened and depressed as it now too often is, either on the one hand by luxurious superfluities, or on the other by the absence of the commonest necessities and the gnawing anxiety for the means of livelihood; not to speak of the everyday uglinesses to which we have accustomed our eyes, confused by the flood of false taste, or darkened by the hurried life of modern towns in which huge aggregations of humanity exist, equally removed from both art and nature and their kindly and refining influences.

It asserts, moreover, the value of the practice of handicraft as a good training for the faculties, and as a most valuable counteraction to that overstraining of purely mental effort under the fierce competitive conditions of the day; apart from the very wholesome and real pleasure in the fashioning of a thing with claims to art and beauty, the struggle with and triumph over the stubborn technical necessities which refuse to be gainsaid. And, finally, thus claiming for man this primitive and common delight in common things made beautiful, it makes, through art, the great socialiser for a common and kindred life, for sympathetic and helpful fellowship, and demands conditions under which your artist and craftsman shall be free.

"See how great a matter a little fire kindleth." Some may think this is an extensive programme—a remote ideal for a purely artistic movement to touch. Yet if the revival of art and handicraft is not a mere theatric and imitative impulse; if it is not merely to gratify a passing whim of fashion, or demand of commerce; if it has reality and roots of its own; if it is not merely a delicate luxury—a little glow of colour at the end of a sombre day—it can hardly mean less than what I have written. It must mean either the sunset or the dawn.

The success which had hitherto attended the efforts of our Society, the sympathy and response elicited by the claims which had been advanced by us on behalf of the Arts and Crafts of Design, and (despite difficulties and imperfections) I think it may be said the character of our exhibitions, and last, but not least, the public interest and support, manifested in various ways, and from different parts of the country, went far to prove both their necessity and importance.

We were therefore encouraged to open a third Exhibition in the autumn of 1890. In this last it was the Society's object to make in it leading features of two crafts in which good design and handicraft are of the utmost importance, namely, Furniture and Embroidery; and endeavours were made to get together good examples of each.

It may be noted that while some well-known firms, who had hitherto held aloof, now exhibited with us, the old difficulty about the names of the responsible executants continued; but while some evaded the question, others were models of exactitude in this respect, proving that in this as in other questions where there is a will there is a way.

The Arts and Crafts Exhibition Society, while at first, of necessity, depending on the work of a comparatively limited circle, had no wish to be narrower than the recognition of certain fundamental principles in design will allow, and, indeed, desired but to receive and to show the *best* after its kind in contemporary design and handicraft. Judgment is not always infallible, and the best is not always forthcoming, and in a mixed exhibition it is difficult to maintain an unvarying standard. At present, indeed, an exhibition may be said to be but a necessary evil; but it is the only means of obtaining a standard, and giving publicity to the works of Designer and Craftsman; but it must be more or less of a compromise, and of course no more can be done than to make an exhibition of contemporary work representative of current ideas and skill, since it is impossible to get outside our own time.

In some quarters it appears to have been supposed that our Exhibitions are intended to appeal, by the exhibition of cheap and saleable articles, to what are rudely termed "the masses"; we appeal to *all* certainly, but it should be remembered that cheapness in art and handicraft is well-nigh impossible, save in some forms of more or less mechanical reproduction. In fact, cheapness as a rule, in the sense of low-priced production, can only be obtained at the cost of cheapness—that is, the cheapening of human life and labour; surely, in reality, a most wasteful and extravagant cheapness! It is difficult to see how, under present economic conditions, it can be otherwise. Art is, in its true sense, after all, the crown and flowering of life and labour, and we cannot reasonably expect to gain that crown except at the true value of the human life and labour of which it is the result.

Of course there is the difference of cost between materials to be taken into account: a table may be of oak or of deal; a cloth may be of silk or of linen; but the labour, skill, taste, intelligence, thought, and fancy, which give the sense of art to the work, are much the same, and, being bound up with human lives, need the means of life in its completion for their proper sustenance.

At all events, I think it may be said that the principle of the essential unity and interdependence of the arts has been again asserted—the brotherhood of designer and craftsman; that goes for something, with whatever imperfections or disadvantages its acknowledgment may have been obscured.

In putting this principle before the public, the Arts and Crafts Exhibition Society has availed itself from the first of both lecture and essay, as well as the display of examples. Lectures and demonstrations were given during the progress of the Exhibitions, and essays written by well-known workers in the crafts of which they treated have accompanied the catalogues. These papers have now been collected together, and revised by their authors, and appear in book form under the editorship of Mr. William Morris, whose name has been practically associated with the revival of beauty in the arts and crafts of design in many ways before our Society came into existence, and who with his co-workers may be said to have been the pioneer of our English Renascence, which it is our earnest desire to foster and perpetuate.

Every movement which has any substance and vitality must expect to encounter misrepresentation, and even abuse, as well as sympathy and support. In its work, so far, the Society to which I have the honour to belong has had its share of both, perhaps.

Those pledged to the support of existing conditions, whether in art or social life, are always sensitive to attacks upon their weak points, and it is not possible to avoid touching them to any man who ventures to look an inch or two beyond the immediate present. But the hostility of some is as much a mark of vitality and progress as the sympathy of others. The sun strikes hottest as the traveller climbs the hill; and we must be content to leave the value of our work to the unfailing test of time.

WALTER CRANE.

TEXTILES

THERE are several ways of ornamenting a woven cloth: (1) real tapestry, (2) carpet-weaving, (3) mechanical weaving, (4) printing or painting, and (5) embroidery. There has been no improvement (indeed, as to the main processes, no change) in the manufacture of the wares in all these branches since the fourteenth century, as far as the wares themselves are concerned; whatever improvements have been introduced have been purely commercial, and have had to do merely with reducing the cost of production; nay, more, the commercial improvements have on the whole been decidedly injurious to the quality of the wares themselves.

The noblest of the weaving arts is Tapestry, in which there is nothing mechanical: it may be looked upon as a mosaic of pieces of colour made up of dyed threads, and is capable of producing wall ornament of any degree of elaboration within the proper limits of duly considered decorative work.

As in all wall-decoration, the first thing to be considered in the designing of Tapestry is the force, purity, and elegance of the *silhouette* of the objects represented, and nothing vague or indeterminate is admissible. But special excellences can be expected from it. Depth of tone, richness of colour, and exquisite gradation of tints are easily to be obtained in Tapestry; and it also demands that crispness and abundance of beautiful detail which was the especial characteristic of fully developed Mediæval Art. The style of even the best period of the Renaissance is wholly unfit for Tapestry: accordingly we find that Tapestry retained its Gothic character longer than any other of the pictorial arts. A comparison of the wall-hangings in the Great Hall at Hampton Court with those in the Solar or Drawing-room, will make this superiority of the earlier design for its purpose clear to any one not lacking in artistic perception: and the comparison is all the fairer, as both the Gothic tapestries of the Solar and the post-Gothic hangings of the Hall are pre-eminently good of their kinds. Not to go into a description of the process of weaving tapestry, which would be futile without illustrations, I may say that in contradistinction to mechanical weaving, the warp is quite hidden, with the result that the colours are as solid as they can be made in painting.

Carpet-weaving is somewhat of the nature of Tapestry: it also is wholly unmechanical, but its use as a floor-cloth somewhat degrades it, especially in our northern or western countries, where people come out of the muddy streets into rooms without taking off their shoes. Carpet-weaving undoubtedly arose among peoples living a tent life, and for such a dwelling as a tent, carpets are the best possible ornaments.

Carpets form a mosaic of small squares of worsted, or hair, or silk threads, tied into a coarse canvas, which is made as the work progresses. Owing to the comparative coarseness of the work, the designs should always be very elementary in form, and *suggestive* merely of forms of leafage, flowers, beasts and birds, etc. The soft gradations of tint to which Tapestry lends itself are unfit for Carpet-weaving; beauty and variety of colour must be attained by harmonious juxtaposition of tints, bounded by judiciously chosen outlines; and the pattern should lie absolutely flat upon the ground. On the whole, in designing carpets the method of *contrast* is the best one to employ, and blue and red, quite frankly used, with white or very light outlines on a dark ground, and black or some very dark colour on a light ground, are the main colours on which the designer should depend.

In making the above remarks I have been thinking only of the genuine or hand-made carpets. The mechanically-made carpets of to-day must be looked upon as makeshifts for cheapness' sake. Of these, the velvet pile and Brussels are simply coarse worsted velvets woven over wires like other velvet, and cut, in the case of the velvet pile; and Kidderminster carpets are stout cloths, in which abundance of warp (a warp to each weft) is used for the sake of wear and tear. The velvet carpets need the same kind of design as to colour and quality as the real carpets; only, as the colours are necessarily limited in number, and the pattern must repeat at certain distances, the design should be simpler and smaller than in a real carpet. A Kidderminster carpet calls for a small design in which the different planes, or plies, as they are called, are well interlocked.

Mechanical weaving has to repeat the pattern on the cloth within comparatively narrow limits; the number of colours also is limited in most cases to four or five. In most cloths so woven, therefore, the best plan seems to be to choose a pleasant ground colour and to superimpose a pattern mainly composed of either a lighter shade of that colour, or a colour in no very strong contrast to the ground; and then, if you are using several colours, to light up this general arrangement either with a more forcible outline, or by spots of stronger colour carefully disposed. Often the lighter shade on the darker suffices, and hardly calls for anything else: some very beautiful cloths are merely damasks, in which the warp and weft are of the same colour, but a different tone is obtained by the figure and the ground being woven with a longer or shorter twill: the *tabby* being tied by the warp very often, the *satin* much more rarely. In any case, the patterned webs produced by mechanical weaving, if the ornament is to be effective and worth the doing, require that same Gothic crispness and clearness of detail which has been spoken of before: the geometrical structure of the pattern, which is a necessity in all recurring patterns, should be boldly insisted upon, so as to draw the eye from accidental figures, which the recurrence of the pattern is apt to produce.

The meaningless stripes and spots and other tormentings of the simple twill of the web, which are so common in the woven ornament of the eighteenth century and in our own times, should be carefully avoided: all these things are the last resource of a jaded invention and a contempt of the simple and fresh beauty that comes of a sympathetic *suggestion* of natural forms: if the pattern be vigorously and firmly drawn with a true feeling for the beauty of line and *silhouette*, the play of light and

Textiles. shade on the material of the simple twill will give all the necessary variety. I invite my readers to make another comparison: to go to the South Kensington Museum and study the invaluable fragments of the stuffs of the thirteenth and fourteenth centuries of Syrian and Sicilian manufacture, or the almost equally beautiful webs of Persian design, which are later in date, but instinct with the purest and best Eastern feeling; they may also note the splendid stuffs produced mostly in Italy in the later Middle Ages, which are unsurpassed for richness and *effect* of design, and when they have impressed their minds with the productions of this great historic school, let them contrast with them the work of the vile Pompadour period, passing by the early seventeenth century as a period of transition into corruption. They will then (if, once more, they have real artistic perception) see at once the difference between the results of irrepressible imagination and love of beauty, on the one hand, and, on the other, of restless and weary vacuity of mind, forced by the exigencies of fashion to do something or other to the innocent surface of the cloth in order to distinguish it in the market from other cloths; between the handiwork of the free craftsman doing as he *pleased* with his work, and the drudgery of the "operative" set to his task by the tradesman competing for the custom of a frivolous public, which had forgotten that there was such a thing as art.

The next method of ornamenting cloth is by painting it or printing on it with dyes. As to the painting of cloths with dyes by hand, which is no doubt a very old and widely practised art, it has now quite disappeared (modern society not being rich enough to pay the necessary price for such work), and its place has now been taken by printing by block or cylinder-machine. The remarks made on the design for mechanically woven cloths apply pretty much to these printed stuffs: only, in the first place, more play of delicate and pretty colour is possible, and more variety of colour also; and in the second, much more use can be made of hatching and dotting, which are obviously suitable to the method of block-printing. In the many-coloured printed cloths, frank red and blue are again the mainstays of the colour arrangement; these colours, softened by the paler shades of red, outlined with black and made more tender by the addition of yellow in small quantities, mostly forming part of brightish greens, make up the colouring of the old Persian prints, which carry the art as far as it can be carried.

It must be added that no textile ornament has suffered so much as cloth-printing from those above-mentioned commercial inventions. A hundred years ago the processes for printing on cloth differed little from those used by the Indians and Persians; and even up to within forty years ago they produced colours that were in themselves good enough, however inartistically they might be used. Then came one of the most wonderful and most useless of the inventions of modern Chemistry, that of the dyes made from coal-tar, producing a series of hideous colours, crude, livid—and cheap,—which every person of taste loathes, but which nevertheless we can by no means get rid of until we are able to struggle successfully against the doom of cheap and nasty which has overtaken us.

Textiles. Last of the methods of ornamenting cloth comes Embroidery: of the design for which it must be said that one of its aims should be the exhibition of beautiful material. Furthermore, it is not worth doing unless it is either very copious and rich, or very delicate—or both. For such an art nothing patchy or scrappy, or half-starved, should be done: there is no excuse for doing anything which is not strikingly beautiful; and that more especially as the exuberance of beauty of the work of the East and of Mediæval Europe, and even of the time of the Renaissance, is at hand to reproach us. It may be well here to warn those occupied in Embroidery against the feeble imitations of Japanese art which are so disastrously common amongst us. The Japanese are admirable naturalists, wonderfully skilful draughtsmen, deft beyond all others in mere execution of whatever they take in hand; and also great masters of style within certain narrow limitations. But with all this, a Japanese design is absolutely worthless unless it is executed with Japanese skill. In truth, with all their brilliant qualities as handicraftsmen, which have so dazzled us, the Japanese have no architectural, and therefore no decorative, instinct. Their works of art are isolated and blankly individualistic, and in consequence, unless where they rise, as they sometimes do, to the dignity of a suggestion for a picture (always devoid of human interest), they remain mere wonderful toys, things quite outside the pale of the evolution of art, which, I repeat, cannot be carried on without the architectural sense that connects it with the history of mankind.

To conclude with some general remarks about designing for textiles: the aim should be to combine clearness of form and firmness of structure with the mystery which comes of abundance and richness of detail ; and this is easier of attainment in woven goods than in flat painted decoration and paper-hangings ; because in the former the stuffs usually hang in folds and the pattern is broken more or less, while in the latter it is spread out flat against the wall. Do not introduce any lines or objects which cannot be explained by the structure of the pattern ; it is just this logical sequence of form, this growth which looks as if, under the circumstances, it could not have been otherwise, which prevents the eye wearying of the repetition of the pattern.

Never introduce any shading for the purpose of making an object look round ; whatever shading you use should be used for explanation only, to show what you mean by such and such a piece of drawing ; and even that you had better be sparing of.

Do not be afraid of large patterns; if properly designed they are more restful to the eye than small ones: on the whole, a pattern where the structure is large and the details much broken up is the most useful. Large patterns are not necessarily startling; this comes more of violent relief of the figure from the ground, or inharmonious colouring: beautiful and logical form relieved from the ground by well-managed contrast or gradation, and lying flat on the ground, will never weary the eye. Very small rooms, as well as very large ones, look best ornamented with large patterns, whatever you do with the middling-sized ones.

As final maxims: never forget the material you are working with, and try

Textiles. always to use it for doing what it can do best: if you feel yourself hampered by the material in which you are working, instead of being helped by it, you have so far not learned your business, any more than a would-be poet has, who complains of the hardship of writing in measure and rhyme. The special limitations of the material should be a pleasure to you, not a hindrance: a designer, therefore, should always thoroughly understand the processes of the special manufacture he is dealing with, or the result will be a mere *tour de force*. On the other hand, it is the pleasure in understanding the capabilities of a special material, and using them for suggesting (not imitating) natural beauty and incident, that gives the *raison d'être* of decorative art.

WILLIAM MORRIS.

OF DECORATIVE PAINTING AND DESIGN

THE term Decorative painting implies the existence of painting which is not decorative: a strange state of things for an art which primarily and pre-eminently appeals to the eye. If we look back to the times when the arts and crafts were in their most flourishing and vigorous condition, and dwelt together, like brethren, in unity—say to the fifteenth century—such a distinction did not exist. Painting only differed in its application, and in degree, not in kind. In the painting of a MS., of the panels of a coffer, of a ceiling, a wall, or an altar-piece, the painter was alike—however different his theme and conception—possessed with a paramount impulse to decorate, to make the space or surface he dealt with as lovely to the eye in design and colour as he had skill to do.

The art of painting has, however, become considerably differentiated since those days. We are here in the nineteenth century encumbered with many distinctions in the art. There is obviously much painting which is not decorative, or ornamental in any sense, which has indeed quite other objects. It may be the presentment of the more superficial natural facts, phases, or accidents of light; the pictorial dramatising of life or past history; the pointing of a moral; or the embodiment of romance and poetic thought or symbol. Not but what it is quite possible for a painter to deal with such things and yet to produce a work that shall be decorative.

A picture, of course, may be a piece of decorative art of the most beautiful kind; but to begin with, if it is an easel picture, it is not necessarily related to anything but itself: its painter is not bound to consider anything outside its own dimensions; and, indeed, the practice of holding large and mixed picture-shows has taught him the uselessness of so doing.

Then, too, the demand for literal presentment of the superficial facts or phases of nature often removes the painter and his picture still farther from the architectural, decorative, and constructive artist and the handicraftsman, who are bound to think of plan, and design, and materials—of the adaptation of their work, in short—while the painter

Of Decorative Painting and Design.

seeks only to be an unbiassed recorder of all accidents and sensational conditions of nature and life,—and so we get our illustrated newspapers on a grand scale.

An illustrated newspaper, however, in spite of the skill and enterprise it may absorb, is not somehow a joy for ever; and, after all, if literalism and instantaneous appearances are the only things worth striving for in painting, the photograph beats any painter at that.

If truth is the object of the modern painter of pictures—truth as distinct from or opposed to beauty—beauty is certainly the object of the decorative painter, but beauty not necessarily severed from truth. Without beauty, however, decoration has no reason for existence; indeed it can hardly be said to exist.

Next to beauty, the first essential of a decoration is that it shall be related to its environment, that it shall express or acknowledge the conditions under which it exists. If a fresco on a wall, for instance, it adorns the wall without attempting to look like a hole cut in it through which something is accidentally seen; if a painting on a vase, it acknowledges the convexity of the shape, and helps to express instead of contradicting it; if on a panel in a cabinet or door, it spreads itself in an appropriate filling on an organic plan to cover it; being, in short, ornamental by its very nature, its first business is to ornament.

There exist, therefore, certain definite tests for the work of the decorative artist. Does the design fit its place and material? Is it in scale with its surroundings and in harmony with itself? Is it fair and lovely in colour? Has it beauty and invention? Has it thought and poetic feeling? These are the demands a decorator has to answer, and by his answer he must stand or fall; but such questions show that the scope of decoration is no mean one.

It must be acknowledged that a mixed exhibition does not easily afford the fairest or completest tests of such qualities. An exhibition is at best a compromise, a convenience, a means of comparison, and to enable work to be shown to the public; but of course is, after all, only really and properly exhibited when it is in the place and position and light for which it was destined. The tests by which to judge a designer's work are only complete then.

As the stem and branches to the leaves, flowers, and fruit of a tree, so is design to painting. In decoration one cannot exist without the other, as the beauty of a figure depends upon the well-built and well-proportioned skeleton and its mechanism. You cannot separate a house from its plan and foundations. So it is in decoration; often thought of lightly as something trivial and superficial, a merely aimless combination of curves and colours, or a mere *réchauffé* of the dead languages of art, but really demanding the best thought and capacity of a man; and in the range of its application it is not less comprehensive.

The mural painter is not only a painter, but a poet, historian, dramatist, philosopher. What should we know, how much should we realise, of the ancient world and its life without him, and his brother the architectural sculptor? How would ancient Egypt live without her wall paintings—or Rome, or Pompeii, or Mediæval Italy? How much of beauty as well as of history is contained in the illuminated pages of the books of the Middle Ages!

Of Decorative Painting and Design.

Some modern essays in mural painting show that the habit of mind and method of work fostered by the production of trifles for the picture market is not favourable to monumental painting. Neither the mood nor the skill, indeed, can be grown like a mushroom; such works as the Sistine Chapel, the Stanzi of Raphael, or the Apartimenti Borgia, are the result of long practice through many centuries, and intimate relationship and harmony in the arts, as well as a certain unity of public sentiment.

The true soil for the growth of the painter in this higher sense is a rich and varied external life: familiarity from early youth with the uses of materials and methods, and the hand facility which comes of close and constant acquaintanceship with the tools of the artist, who sums up and includes in himself other crafts, such as modelling, carving, and the hammering of metal, architectural design, and a knowledge of all the ways man has used to beautify and deck the surroundings and accessories of life to satisfy his delight in beauty.

We know that painting was strictly an applied art in its earlier history, and all through the Middle Ages painters were in close alliance with the other crafts of design, and their work in one craft no doubt reacted on and influenced that in another, while each was kept distinct. At all events, painters like Albert Dürer and Holbein were also masters of design in all ways.

Through the various arts and crafts of the Greek, Mediæval, or Early Renaissance periods, there is evident, from the examples which have come down to us, a certain unity and common character in design, asserting itself through all diverse individualities: each art is kept distinct, with a complete recognition of the capacity and advantages of its own particular method and purpose.

In our age, for various reasons (social, commercial, economic), the specialised and purely pictorial painter is dominant. His aims and methods influence other arts and crafts, but by no means advantageously as a rule; since, unchecked by judicious ideas of design, attempts are made in unsuitable materials to produce so-called realistic force, and superficial and accidental appearances dependent on peculiar qualities of lighting and atmosphere, quite out of place in any other method than painting, or in any place but an easel picture.

From such tendencies, such influences as these, in the matter of applied art and design, we are striving to recover. One of the first results is, perhaps, this apparently artificial distinction between decorative and other painting. But along with this we have painters whose easel pictures are in feeling and treatment quite adaptable as wall and panel decorations, and they are painters who, as a rule, have studied other methods in art, and drawn their inspiration from the mode of Mediæval or Early Renaissance times.

Much might be said of different methods and materials of work in decorative painting, but I have hardly space here. The decorative painter prefers a certain flatness of effect, and therefore such methods as fresco, in which the colours are laid on while the plaster ground is wet, and tempera naturally appeal to him. In the latter the colours ground in water and used with size, or white and yolk of egg, or prepared with starch, worked on a dry

Of Decorative Painting and Design.

ground, drying lighter than when they are put on, have a peculiar luminous quality, while the surface is free from any gloss. Both these methods need direct painting and finishing as the work proceeds.

By a method of working in ordinary oil colours on a ground of fibrous plaster, using rectified spirit of turpentine or benzine as a medium, much of the quality of fresco or tempera may be obtained, with the advantage that the plaster ground may be a movable panel.

There are, however, other fields for the decorative painter than wall painting; as, for instance, domestic furniture, which may vary in degree of elaboration from the highly ornate cassone or marriage coffer of Mediæval Italy to the wreaths and sprays which decked chairs and bed-posts even within our century. There has been of late some revival of painting as applied chiefly to the panels of cabinets, or the decoration of piano fronts and cases.

Of Decorative Painting and Design.

The same causes produce the same results. With the search after, and desire for, beauty in life, we are again driven to study the laws of beauty in design and painting; and in so doing painters will find again the lost thread, the golden link of connection and intimate association with the sister arts and handicrafts, whereof none is before or after another, none is greater or less than the other.

WALTER CRANE.

OF WALL PAPERS

WHILE the tradition and practice of mural painting as applied to interior walls and ceilings of houses still linger in Italy, in the form of often skilful if not always tasteful tempera work, in more western countries, like England, France, and America, under the economic conditions and customs of commercial civilisation, with its smoky cities, and its houses built by the hundred to one pattern, perhaps, and let on short terms, as regards domestic decoration—except in the case of a few wealthy freeholders—mural painting has ceased to exist. Its place has been taken by what after all is but a substitute for it, namely, wall paper.

Of Wall Papers.

I am not aware that any specimen of wall paper has been discovered that has claims to any higher antiquity than the sixteenth century, and it only came much into use in the last, increasing in the present, until it has become well-nigh a universal covering for domestic walls, and at the same time has shown a remarkable development in design, varying from very unpretending patterns and printings in one colour to elaborate block-printed designs in many colours, besides cheap machine-printed papers, where all the tints are printed from the design on a roller at once.

Since Mr. William Morris has shown what beauty and character in pattern, and good and delicate choice of tint can do for us, giving in short a new impulse

Of Wall Papers.

in design, a great amount of ingenuity and enterprise has been spent on wall papers in England, and in the better kinds a very distinct advance has been made upon the patterns of inconceivable hideousness, often of French origin, of the period of the Second Empire—a period which perhaps represents the most degraded level of taste in decoration generally.

The designer of patterns for wall papers heretofore has been content to imitate other materials, and adapt the characteristics of the patterns found, say, in silk damask hangings or tapestry, or even imitate the veining of wood, or marble, or tiles; but since the revival of interest in art, the study of its history, and knowledge of style, a new impulse has been given, and patterns are constructed with more direct reference to their beauty, and interest as such, while strictly adapted to the methods of manufacture. Great pains are often taken by our principal makers to secure good designs and harmonious colourings, and though a manufacturer and director of works is always more or less controlled by the exigencies of the market and the demands of the tentative salesman—considerations which have no natural connection with art, though highly important as economic conditions affecting its welfare—very remarkable results have been produced, and a special development of applied design may almost be said to have come into existence with the modern use of wall papers. The manufacture suffers like most others from the keenness and unscrupulousness of commercial competition, which leads to the production of specious imitations of *bonâ fide* designs, and unauthorised use of designs originally intended for other purposes, and this of course presses unfairly upon the more conscientious maker, so long as the public do not decline to be deceived.

English wall papers are made in lengths 21 inches wide. French wall papers are 18 inches wide. This has probably been found most convenient in working in block-printing: it is obvious to any one who has seen the printers at work that a wider block than 21 inches would be unwieldy, since the block is printed by hand, being suspended from above by a cord, and guided by the workman's hand from the well of colour, into which it is dipped, to the paper flat on a table before him.

The designer must work to the given width, and though his design may vary in depth, must never exceed 21 inches square, except where double blocks are used. His main business is to devise his pattern so that it will repeat satisfactorily over an indefinite wall space without running into awkward holes or lines. It may be easy enough to draw a spray or two of leaves or flowers which will stand by themselves, but to combine them in an organic pattern which shall repeat pleasantly over a wall surface requires much ingenuity and a knowledge of the conditions of the manufacture, apart from play of fancy and artistic skill.

One way of concealing the joints of the repeat of the pattern is by contriving what is called a drop-repeat, so that, in hanging, the paper-hanger, instead of placing each repeat of pattern side by side, is enabled to join the pattern at a point its own depth below, which varies the effect, and arranges the chief features or masses on an alternating plan.

The modern habit of regarding the walls of a room chiefly as a background to pictures, furniture, or people, and perhaps the smallness of the average room, has brought rather small, thickly dispersed, leafy patterns into vogue, retiring in colour for the most part. While, however, we used to see rotund and accidental bunches of roses (the pictorial or sketchy treatment of which contrasted awkwardly with their formal repetition), we now get a certain sense of adaptation, and the necessity of a certain flatness of treatment; and most of us who have given much thought to the subject feel that when natural forms are dealt with, under such conditions, suggestion is better than any attempt at realisation, or naturalistic or pictorial treatment, and that a design must be constructed upon some systematic plan, if not absolutely controlled by a geometric basis.

Wall papers are printed from blocks

prepared from designs, the outlines of which are reproduced by means of flat brass wire driven edgeways into the wood block. One block for each tint is used. First one colour is printed on a length of paper, a piece of 12 yards long and 21 inches wide, which is passed over sticks suspended across the workshop. When the first colour is dry the next is printed, and so on; the colours being mixed with size and put in shallow trays or wells, into which the blocks are dipped.

A cheaper kind is printed by steam power from rollers on which the design has been reproduced in the same way by brass wire, which holds the colour; but in the case of machine-printed papers all the tints are printed at once. Thus the pattern is often imperfect and blurred.

A more elaborate and costly kind of

Of Wall Papers.

wall paper is that which is stamped and gilded, in emulation of stamped and gilded leather, which it resembles in effect and quality of surface. For this method the design is reproduced in relief as a *repoussée* brass plate, and from this a mould or matrix is made, and the paper being damped is stamped in a press into the matrix, and so takes the pattern in relief, which is generally covered with white metal and lacquered to a gold hue, and this again may be rubbed in with black, which by filling the interstices gives emphasis to the design and darkens the gold to bronze; or the gilded surface may be treated in any variety of colour by means of painting or lacquer, or simply relieved by colouring the ground.

But few of us own our own walls, or the ground they stand upon: but few of us can afford to employ ourselves or skilled artists and craftsmen in painting our rooms with beautiful fancies: but if we can get well-designed repeating patterns by the yard, in agreeable tints, with a pleasant flavour perchance of nature or antiquity, for a few shillings or pounds, ought we not to be happy? At all events, wall-paper makers should naturally think so.

WALTER CRANE.

FICTILES

EARLIEST amongst the inventions of man and his endeavour to unite Art with Craft is the Fictile Art. His first needs in domestic life, his first utensils, his first efforts at civilisation, came from the Mother Earth, whose son he believed himself to be, and his ashes or his bones returned to Earth enshrined in the fictile vases he created from their common clay. And these Fictiles tell the story of his first Art-instincts, and of his yearnings to unite beauty with use. They tell, too, more of his history than is enshrined and preserved by any other art; for almost all we know of many a people and many a tongue is learned from the fictile record, the sole relic of past civilisations which the Destroyer Time has left us.

Fictiles.

Begun in the simplest fashion, fashioned by the simplest means, created from the commonest materials, Fictile Art grew with man's intellectual growth, and Fictile Craft grew with his knowledge; the latter conquering, in this our day, when the craftsman strangles the artist alike in this as in all other arts. To truly foster and forward the art, the craftsman and the artist should, where possible, be united, or at least should work in common, as was the case when, in each civilisation, the Potter's Art flourished most, and when the scientific base was of less account than was the art employed upon it. In its earliest stages the local clay sufficed for the

Fictiles. formative portion of the work, and the faiences of most European countries offer more artistic results to us than do the more scientifically compounded porcelains. In the former case the native clay seemed more easily to ally itself with native art, to record more of current history, to create artistic genius rather than to be content with attempting to copy misunderstood efforts of other peoples and other times. But when science ransacked the earth for foreign bodies and ingredients, foreign decorative ideas came with them and Fictile Art was no more a vernacular one. It attempted to disguise itself, to show the craftsman superior to the artist; and then came the Manufacturer and the reign of quantity over quality, the casting in moulds by the gross and the printing by the thousands. Be it understood these remarks only apply to the introduction of porcelain into Europe. In the East where the clay is native, the art is native ; the potter's hand and the wheel yet maintain the power of giving the potter his individuality as the creator and the artist, and save him from being but the servant and the slave of a machine.

Between faience and porcelain comes, midway, Stoneware, in which many wonderfully, and some fearfully, made things have been done of late, but which possesses the combined qualities of faience and porcelain — the ease of manipulation of the former, and the hardness and durability of the latter ; but the tendency to over-elaborate the detail of its decoration, and rely less on the beauty of its semi-glossy surface than on meretricious ornament, has rather spoiled a very hopeful movement in Ceramic Art. Probably the wisest course to pursue at the present would be to pay more attention to faiences decorated with simple glazes or with "slip" decoration, and this especially in modelled work. A continuation of the artistic career of the Della Robbia family is yet an unfulfilled desideratum, notwithstanding that glazed faiences have never since their time ceased to be made, and that glazed figure work of large scale prevailed in the eighteenth century. Unglazed terra cotta, an artistic product eminently suited to our climate and to our urban architecture, has but partially developed itself, and this more in the direction of moulded and cast work than that of really plastic art; and albeit that from its dawn to this present the Fictile Art has been exercised abundantly, its rôle is by no means exhausted. The artist and the craftsman have yet a wide field before them, but it would be well that the former should, for some while to come, take the lead. Science has too long reigned supreme in a domain wherein she should have been not more than equal sovereign. She has had her triumphs, great triumphs too, triumphs which have been fraught with good in an utilitarian sense, but she has tyrannised too rigidly over the realm of Art. Let us now try to equalise the dual rule.

G. T. Robinson.

METAL WORK

IN discussing the artistic aspect of metal work, we have to take into account the physical properties and appropriate treatment of the following metals: the precious metals, gold and silver; copper, both pure and alloyed with other metals, especially tin and zinc in various proportions to form the many kinds of brass and bronze; lead, with a group of alloys of which pewter is typical; and iron, in the three forms of cast iron, wrought iron, and steel. All these have been made to serve the purpose of the artist, and the manipulation of them, while presenting many differences in detail, presents certain broad characteristics in common which distinguish them from the raw material of other crafts. Whether they are found native in the metallic state as is usual in the case of gold, or combined with many other minerals in the form of ore as is more common with other metals, fire is the primal agency by which they are made available for our needs. The first stage in their manipulation is to melt and cast them into ingots of a size convenient to the purpose intended. Secondly, all these metals when pure, and many alloys, are in varying degree malleable and ductile, are, in fact, if sufficient force be applied, plastic. Hence arises the first broad division in the treatment of metals. The fluid metal may, by the use of suitable moulds, be cast at once to the shape required, or the casting may be treated merely as the starting-point for a whole series of operations—forging, rolling, chipping, chasing, wire-drawing, and many more. Another property of the metals which must be noticed is, that not only can separate masses of metals be melted down and fused into one, but it is possible, under various conditions, of which the one invariably necessary is perfectly clean surfaces of contact, to unite separate portions of the same or different metals without fusion of the mass. For our present purpose the most important instance of this is the process of soldering, by which two surfaces are united by the application of sufficient heat to melt more fusible metal which is introduced between them, and which combines with both so as firmly to unite them on solidifying. Closely allied to this are the processes by which one metal is, for purposes of adornment or preservation from corrosion, coated with a thin film or deposit of another, usually more costly, metal.

Though hereafter electro-metallurgy may assert its claim to artistic originality as a third division, for the present all metal work, so far as its artistic aspect depends upon process, falls naturally into one of the two broad divisions of cast metal and wrought metal. Both have been employed from a time long anterior to written history; ornaments of beaten gold, and tools of cast bronze, are alike found among the relics of very early stages of civilisation, and in early stages both alike are artistic. The choice between the two processes is determined by such considerations as convenience of manufacture and the physical properties of the metals, and the different purposes in view. When

Metal Work. a thick and comparatively massive shape is required, it is often easier to cast it at once. For thinner and lighter forms it is usually more convenient to treat the ingot or crude product of the furnace as mere raw material for a long series of workings under the hammer, or its patent mechanical equivalents, the rolling and pressing mills of modern mechanics. The choice is further influenced by the toughness generally characteristic of wrought metal, whereas the alloys which yield the cleanest castings are by no means universally the best in other respects. Iron is the extreme instance of this: ordinary cast iron being an impure form of the metal, which is too brittle to be worked under the hammer, but is readily cast into moulds, being fluid at a temperature which, though high, is easily obtained in a blast furnace. Wrought iron, however, which is usually obtained from cast iron by a process called puddling, whereby the impurities are burnt out, does not become fluid enough to pour into moulds; but on the other hand, pieces at a white heat can be united into a solid mass by skilful hammering, a process which is called welding, and, together with the fact that from its great hardness it is usually worked hot, is specially distinctive of the blacksmith's craft. In no other metal is the separation between the two branches so wide as in iron. The misdirected skill of some modern iron-founders has caused the name of cast iron to be regarded as the very negative of art, and has even thrown suspicion on the process of casting itself as one of questionable honesty. Nevertheless, as a craft capable of giving final shape to metal, it has manifestly an artistic aspect, and, in fact, bronze statuary, a fine art pure and simple, is reproduced from the clay model merely by moulding and casting. We must therefore look for the artistic conditions in the preparation of the model or pattern, the impress of which in sand or loam forms the mould; the pattern may be carved in wood or modelled in clay, but the handling of the wood or clay is modified by the conditions under which the form is reproduced. And lastly, the finished object may either retain the surface formed as the metal solidifies, as in the case of the bronzes cast by the wax process, or the skin may be removed by the use of cutting tools, chisels and files and gravers, so that, as in the case of many of the better French bronzes, the finished work is strictly carved work. On the contrary, much silversmith's work, as well as such simple objects as Chinese gongs and Indian "lotahs," after being cast approximately to shape are finished by hammer work, that is, treated as plastic material with tools that force the material into shape instead of cutting the shape out of the mass by removing exterior portions of material. Attempts to imitate both processes by casting only, thus dispensing with the cost of finishing, are common, but as they dispense likewise with all beauty in the product, even if they do not substitute varnished and tinted zinc for better metal, their success is commercial only.

We have thus three characteristic kinds of surface resulting from the conditions of treatment, marking out three natural divisions of the art: and be it noted that questions of surface or texture are all-important in the arts; beauty is skin deep. First, the natural skin of the metal solidified in contact

Metal Work. with the mould, and more or less closely imitative of the surface of the original model, usually for our purposes a plastic surface; secondly, there is carved, technically called chased, work; and thirdly, beaten or wrought work, which in ornament is termed embossing.

Superimposed on these we have the cross divisions of the crafts according to the special metal operated on, and in the existing industrial organisation the groups thus obtained have to be further divided into many sub-heads, according to the articles produced; and finally, another commercial distinction has to be drawn which greatly affects the present condition of handicraft, that is, the division of the several trades into craftsmen and salesmen. There can be no doubt that the extent of the existing dissociation of the producing craftsman from the consumer is an evil for the arts, and that the growing preponderance of great stores is inimical to excellence of workmanship. It is, perhaps, an advantage for the workman to be relieved from the office of salesman; the position of the village smith plying his calling in face of his customers might not suit every craft, but the services of the middleman are dearly bought at the price of artistic freedom. It is too often in the power of the middleman to dictate the quality of workmanship, too often his seeming interest to ordain that it shall be bad.

The choice of a metal for any particular purpose is determined by physical properties combined with considerations of cost. Iron, if only for its cheapness, is the material for the largest works of metal; while in the form of steel it is the best available material for many very small works, watch-springs for instance:

Metal Work. it has the defect of liability to rust ; the surfaces of other metals may tarnish, but iron rusts through. For the present only one application of cast iron concerns us—its use for grates and stoves. The point to remember is, that as the material has but little beauty, its employment should be restricted to the quantity prescribed by the demands of utility. Wrought iron, on the contrary, gives very great scope to the artist, and it offers this peculiar advantage, that the necessity of striking while the iron is hot enforces such free dexterity of handling in the ordinary smith, that he has comparatively little to learn if set to produce ornamental work, and thus renewed interest in the art has found craftsmen enough who could readily respond to the demand made upon them.

Copper, distinguished among metals

by its glowing red tint, has as a material for artistic work been overshadowed by its alloys, brass and bronze; partly because they make sounder castings, partly it is to be feared from the approach of their colour to gold. Holding an intermediate position between iron and the precious metals, they are the material of innumerable household utensils and smaller architectural fittings.

Lead, tin, and zinc scarcely concern the artist to-day, though neither plumber nor pewterer has always been restricted to plain utilitarianism. Gold and silver have been distinguished in all ages as the precious metals, both for their comparative rarity and their freedom from corrosion, and their extreme beauty. They are both extremely malleable and very readily worked. Unhappily there is little original English work being done in these metals. The

Metal Work. more ordinary wares have all life and feeling taken out of them by mechanical finish, an abrasive process being employed to remove every sign of tool-marks. The all-important surface is thus obliterated. As to design, fashion oscillates between copies of one past period and another. A comparison of one of these copies with an original will make the distinction between the work of a man paid to do his quickest and one paid to do his best clearer than volumes of description. Indeed, when all is said, a writer can but indicate the logic that underlies the craft, or hint at the relation which subsists between the process, the material, and the finished ware: the distinction between good and bad in art eludes definition; it is not an affair of reason, but of perception.

W. A. S. Benson.

STONE AND WOOD CARVING

THE crafts of the stone and wood carver may fairly be taken in review at the same time, although they differ in themselves.

It is a misfortune that there should be so great a gulf as there is between the craftsman who is called, and considers himself to be properly called, "a sculptor" and his fellow-craftsman who is called "a carver." In these days the "sculptor" is but too often a man who would think it a condescension to execute what, for want of a better name, we must call decorative work. In truth, the sculptor is the outcome of that entire separation which has come about between the love of beauty, once common in everyday life, and art, as it is now called—a thing degraded to the purposes of a toy, a mere ornament for the rich. The sculptor is trained to make these ornaments, things which have no relation to their surroundings, but which may be placed now in a drawing-room, now in a conservatory or a public square, alone and unsheltered. He is a child of the studio.

The result of this training is, he has lost all knowledge how to produce work of a decorative character. He understands nothing of design in a wide sense, but being able to model a figure with tolerable success he rests therewith content. Being designed, as it is, in the studio, his work is wanting in sympathy with its surroundings; it does not fall into its place, it is not a part of a complete conception.

Things were not so when sculpture and what, for want of a better term, we have called "stone and wood carving" were at their prime.

The Greek craftsman could produce both the great figure of the god, which stood alone as the central object in the temple, and (working in thorough sympathy with the architect) the decorative sculpture of less importance which was attached to the building round about, and without which the beauty of the fabric was incomplete.

So also the great Florentine sculptors spent themselves with equal zeal on a door, the enclosure of a choir, a pulpit, or a tomb, which in those days meant not merely the effigy of the departed, but a complete design of many parts all full of beauty and skill.

Stone and Wood Carving.

In the great days of Mediæval Art sculpture played a part of the highest importance. The works then produced are not only excellent in themselves, but are so designed as to form a part of the building they adorn. How thoroughly unfinished would be the west front of the Cathedral at Wells, or the portals of Amiens or Reims, without their sculpture.

How rarely can we feel this sense of satisfaction, of unity of result, between the work of the sculptor and the architect in our buildings of to-day. The figures are "stood about" like ornaments on the mantelpiece. The architect seems as unable to prepare for them as the sculptor to make them. We seldom see congruity even between the figure and the pedestal on which it stands.

The want of this extended sympathy leads to another ill result. Wood, stone, and metal, different as they are, are treated by the artist in much the same fashion. The original model in clay seems to stand behind everything. The "artist" makes the clay model; his subordinates work it out in one or another material. The result can only be unsatisfactory because the natural limitations fixed by the qualities of the different materials have been neglected, whereas they should stand forth prominently in the mind of the artist from the moment he first conceives his design.

Stone and Wood Carving.

Marble, stones—some hard, some soft,—terra cotta, metals, or wood, each demand a difference of treatment. For example, the fibrous nature of wood enables the craftsman to produce work which would fall to pieces at the first blow if executed in stone. The polished and varied surface of marble demands a treatment of surface and section of mouldings which

Stone and Wood Carving.

in stone would seem tame and poor. Again, it must not be forgotten that most works in stone or marble are built up. They are composed of many blocks standing one on the other. With wood it is quite different. Used in thick pieces it splits; good wood-work is therefore framed together, the framing and intermediate panelling lending itself to the richest decoration; but anything in the design which suggests stone construction is obviously wrong. In short, wood must be treated as a material that is fibrous and tenacious, and in planks or slabs; stone or marble as of close, even texture, brittle and in blocks.

Consequent on these differences of texture, we find that the tools and method of handling them used by the wood-carver differ in many respects from those used by the worker in stone or marble.

One material is scooped and cut out, the other is attacked by a constant repetition of blows.

Stone and Wood Carving.

In the history of Mediæval Art we find that the craft of the stone-carver was perfectly understood long before that of his brother craftsman in wood. Whilst the first had all through Europe attained great perfection in the thirteenth century, the second did not reach the same standard till the fifteenth, and with the classic revival it died out. Nothing displays more fully the adaptation of design and decoration to the material than much of the fifteenth-century stall-work in our English cathedrals. These could only be executed in wood; the design is suited to that material only; but when the Italian influence creeps in, the designs adopted are in fact suited to fine stone, marble, or alabaster, and not to wood.

Stone and Wood Carving.

Until the craftsman in stone and wood is more of an architect, and the architect more of a craftsman, we cannot hope for improvement.

SOMERS CLARKE.

FURNITURE

THE institution of schools of art and design, and the efforts of serials and magazines devoted to artistic matters, have had their proper effect in the creation of a pretty general distaste for the clumsy and inartistic forms which characterised cabinets and furniture generally some years back. Unfortunately for the movement, some manufacturers saw their opportunity in the demand thus created for better and more artistic shapes to produce bad and ill-made copies of good designs, which undermined the self-respect of the

Furniture. unfortunate man (frequently a good and sufficient craftsman) whose ill hap it was to be obliged to make them, and vexed the soul of the equally unfortunate purchaser.

The introduction of machinery for moulding, which left only the fitting and polishing to be done by the craftsman, and which enabled manufacturers to produce two or three cabinets in the time formerly occupied in the making of one, was all against the quality and stability of the work. No good work was ever done in a hurry : the craftsman may be rapid, but his rapidity is the result of very deliberate thought, and not of hurry. Good furniture, however, cannot be made rapidly. All wood, no matter how long it is kept, nor how dry it may be superficially, will always shrink again when cut into.

It follows that the longer the interval

between the cutting up of the wood, and its fitting together, the better for the work. In the old times the parts of a cabinet lay about in the workman's benchway for weeks, and even months, and were continually turned over and handled by him while he was engaged on the mouldings and other details. The wood thus became really dry, and no further shrinkage could take place after it was put together.

A word here about the designing of cabinets.

Modern furniture designers are far too much influenced by considerations of style, and sacrifice a good deal that is valuable in order to conform to certain rules which, though sound enough in their relation to architecture, do not really apply to furniture at all. Much more pleasing, and not necessarily less artistic work would be produced, were

Furniture. designers, and handicraftsmen too, encouraged to allow their imagination more scope, and to get more of their own individuality into their work, instead of being the slaves of styles invented by people who lived under quite different conditions from those now prevailing.

Mouldings as applied to cabinets are nearly always too coarse, and project too much. This applies equally to the carvings, which should always be quite subordinate to the general design and mouldings, and (in its application to surfaces) should be in low relief. This is quite compatible with all necessary vigour as well as refinement. The idea that boldness—viz. high projection of parts in carving—has anything to do with vigour is a common one, but is quite erroneous. All the power and vigour which he is capable of putting into anything, the clever carver can put into a piece of ornament which shall not project more than a quarter of an inch from the ground in any part. Indeed, I have known good carvers who did their best work within those limits.

Knowledge of line, of the management of planes, with dexterity in the handling of surfaces, is all he requires. Another common mistake is to suppose that smoothness of surface has anything to do with finish properly so called. If only half the time which is commonly spent in smoothing and polishing carved surfaces was devoted to the more thorough study and development of the various parts of the design, and the correction of the outlines, the surface might very well be left to take care of itself, and the work would be the better for it.

There is not space in this paper to do more than glance at a few other

Furniture. methods in ordinary use for cabinet decoration. Marquetry, inlays of ivory, and various other materials have always been extensively used, and sometimes with excellent effect. In many old examples the surface of the solid wood was cut away to the pattern, and various other kinds of wood pressed into the lines so sunk. The method more generally adopted now is to insert the pattern into veneer which has been prepared to receive it, and mount the whole on a solid panel or shape with glue.

The besetting sin of the modern designer or maker of marquetry is a tendency to "loud" colour and violent contrasts of both colour and grain. It is common to see as many as a dozen different kinds of wood used in the decoration of a modern cabinet—some of them stained woods, and the colours of no two of them in harmony.

The best work in this kind depends for its effect on a rich, though it may be low tone of colour. It is seldom that more than two or three different kinds of wood are used, but each kind is so carefully selected for the purpose of the design, and is used in so many different ways, that, while the all-important "tone" is kept throughout, the variety of surface is almost infinite. For this reason, though it is not necessary that the designer should actually cut the work himself, it is most essential that he should always be within call of the cutter, and should himself select every piece of wood which is introduced into the design. This kind of work is sometimes shaded with hot sand; at other times a darker wood is introduced into the pattern for the shadows. The latter is the better way; the former is the cheaper.

Furniture.

Furniture.

The polishing of cabinet work. I have so strong an objection in this connection to the French polisher and all his works and ways, that, notwithstanding the popular prejudice in favour of brilliant surfaces, I would have none of him. Formerly the cabinetmaker was accustomed to polish his own work, sometimes by exposing the finished surfaces to the light for a few weeks in order to darken them, and then applying beeswax with plentiful rubbing. This was the earliest and the best method, but in later times a polish composed of naphtha and shellac was used. The latter polish, though open to many of the objections which may be urged against that now in use, was at least hard and lasting, which can hardly be said of its modern substitute.

The action of the more reputable cabinetmaking firms has been, of late, almost wholly in the direction of better design and construction; but a still better guarantee of progress in the future of the craft is found in the fact that the craftsman who takes an artistic and intelligent, and not a merely mechanical interest in his work, is now often to be met. To such men greater individual freedom is alone wanting.

Furniture.

STEPHEN WEBB.

STAINED GLASS

IN these days there is a tendency to judge the merits of stained glass from the standpoint of the archæologist. It is good or bad in so far as it is directly imitative of work of the fourteenth or fifteenth century. The art had reached to a surprising degree of beauty and perfection in the fifteenth century, and although under the influence of the Renaissance some good work was done, it rapidly declined only to lift its head once more with the revived study of the architecture of the Middle Ages.

The burning energy of Pugin, which

nothing could escape, was directed towards this end, but the attainment of a mere archæological correctness was the chief aim in view. The crude draughtsmanship of the ancient craftsman was diligently imitated, but the spirit and charm of the original was lost, as, in a mere imitation, it must be. In the revival of the art, whilst there was an attempt to imitate the drawing, there was no attempt to reproduce the quality of the ancient glass. Thus, brilliant, transparent, and unbroken tints were used, lacking all the richness and splendour of colour so characteristic of the originals. Under these conditions of blind imitation the modern worker in stained glass produced things probably more hideous than the world ever saw before.

Departing altogether from the traditions of the mediæval schools, whether ancient or modern, there has arisen another school which has found its chief exponents at Munich. The object of these people has been, ignoring the condition under which they must necessarily work, to produce an ordinary picture in enamelled colours upon sheets of glass. The result has been the production of mere transparencies no better than painted blinds.

What then, it may be asked, are the limiting conditions, imposed upon him by the nature of the materials, within which the craftsman must work to produce a satisfactory result?

In the first place, a stained glass window is not an easel picture. It does not stand within a frame, as does the easel picture, in isolation from the objects surrounding it; it is not even an object to be looked at by itself; its duty is, not only to be beautiful, but to play its part in the adornment of the building in which it is placed, being subordinated to the effect the interior is intended to produce as a whole. It is, in fact, but one of many parts that go to *produce a complete result*. A visit to one of our mediæval churches, such as York Minster, Gloucester Cathedral, or Malvern Priory, church buildings, which still retain much of their ancient glass, and a comparison of the unity of effect there experienced with the internecine struggle exhibited in most buildings furnished by the glass painters of to-day, will surely convince the most indifferent that there is yet much to be learned.

Secondly, the great difference between coloured glass and painted glass must be kept in view. A coloured glass window is in the nature of a mosaic. Not only are no large pieces of glass used, but each piece is separated from and at the same time joined to its neighbour by a thin grooved strip of lead which holds the two. "*Coloured glass* is obtained by a mixture of metallic oxides whilst in a state of fusion. This colouring pervades the substance of the glass and becomes incorporated with it."[1] It is termed "pot-metal." An examination of such a piece of glass will show it to be full of varieties of a given colour, uneven in thickness, full of little air-bubbles and other accidents which cause the rays of light to play in and through it with endless variety of effect. It is the exact opposite to the clear sheet of ordinary window-glass.

To build up a decorative work (and such a form of expression may be found very appropriate in this craft) in coloured

[1] *Industrial Arts*, "Historical Sketches," p. 195, published for the Committee of Council on Education. Chapman and Hall.

glass, the pieces must be carefully selected, the gradations of tint in a given piece being made use of to gain the result aimed at. The leaded "canes" by which the whole is held together are made use of to aid the effect. Fine lines and hatchings are painted as with "silver stain," and in this respect only is there any approach to enamelling in the making of a coloured glass window. The glass mosaic as above described is held in its place in the window by horizontal iron bars, and the position of these is a matter of some importance, and is by no means overlooked by the artist in considering the effect of his finished work. A well-designed coloured glass window is, in fact, like nothing else in the world but itself. It is not only a mosaic; it is not merely a picture. It is the honest outcome of the use of glass for making a beautiful window which shall transmit light and not look like anything but what it is. The effect of the work is obtained by the contrast of the rich colours of the pot-metal with the pearly tones of the clear glass.

We must now describe a *painted* window, so that the distinction between a coloured and a painted window may be clearly made out. Quoting from the same book as before—"To paint glass the artist uses a plate of translucent glass, and applies the design and colouring with vitrifiable colours. These colours, true enamels, are the product of metallic oxides combined with vitreous compounds called fluxes. Through the medium of these, assisted by a strong heat, the colouring matters are fixed upon the plate of glass." In the painted window we are invited to forget that glass is being used. Shadows are obtained by loading the surface with enamel colours; the fullest rotundity of modelling is aimed at; the lead and iron so essentially necessary to the construction and safety of the window are concealed with extraordinary skill and ingenuity. The spectator perceives a hole in the wall with a very indifferent picture in it—overdone in the high lights, smoky and unpleasant in the shadows, in no sense decorative. We need concern ourselves no more with painted windows; they are thoroughly false and unworthy of consideration.

Of coloured or stained windows, as they are more commonly called, many are made, mostly bad, but there are amongst us a few who know how to make them well, and these are better than any made elsewhere in Europe at this time.

SOMERS CLARKE.

TABLE GLASS

FEW materials lend themselves more readily to the skill of the craftsman than glass. The fluid or viscous condition of the "metal" as it comes from the "pot," the way in which it is shaped by the breath of the craftsman, and by his skill in making use of centrifugal force, these and many other things too numerous to mention are all manifested in the triumphs of the Venetian glass-blower. At the first glance we see that the vessel he has made is of a material once liquid. He takes the fullest advantage of the conditions under which he works, and the result is a beautiful thing which can be produced in but one way.

For many centuries the old methods were followed, but with the power to produce the "metal," or glass of extreme purity and transparency, came the desire to leave the old paths, and produce work in imitation of crystal. The wheel came into play, and cut and engraved glass became general. At first there was nothing but a genuine advance or variation on the old modes.

The specimens of clear glass made at the end of the seventeenth and beginning of the eighteenth centuries are well designed to suit the capabilities of the material. The form given to the liquid metal by the craftsman's skill is still manifest, its delicate transparency accentuated here and there by cutting the surface into small facets, or engraving

Table Glass. upon it graceful designs ; but as skill increased so taste degraded. The graceful outlines and natural curves of the old workers gave place to distortions of line but too common in all decorative works of the period. A little later and the material was produced in mere lumps, cut and tormented into a thousand surfaces, suggesting that the work was made from the solid, as, in part, it was. This miserable stuff reached its climax in the early years of the present reign.

Since then a great reaction has taken place. For example, the old decanter, a massive lump of misshapen material better suited to the purpose of braining a burglar than decorating a table, has given place to a light and gracefully formed vessel, covered in many cases with well-designed surface engraving, and thoroughly suited both to the uses it

is intended to fulfil and the material of
which it is made. And not only so, but a distinct variation and development upon the old types has been made. The works produced have not been merely copies, but they have their own character. It is not necessary to describe the craft of the glass-blower. It is sufficient to say that he deals with a material which, when it comes to his hands, is a liquid, solidifying rapidly on exposure to the air; that there is hardly a limit to the delicacy of the film that can be made; and, in addition to using a material of one colour, different colours can be laid one over the other, the outer ones being afterwards cut through by the wheel, leaving a pattern in one colour on a ground of another.

There has developed itself of late an unfortunate tendency to stray from the

Table Glass. path of improvement,[1] but a due consideration on the part both of the purchaser and of the craftsman of how the material should be used will result, it may be hoped, in farther advances on the right road.

SOMERS CLARKE.

[1] Novelty rather than improvement is the rock on which our craftsmen are but too often wrecked.

PRINTING

PRINTING, in the only sense with which we are at present concerned, differs from most if not from all the arts and crafts represented in the Exhibition in being comparatively modern. For although the Chinese took impressions from wood blocks engraved in relief for centuries before the wood-cutters of the Netherlands, by a similar process, produced the block books, which were the immediate predecessors of the true printed book, the invention of movable metal letters in the middle of the fifteenth century may justly be considered

Printing. as the invention of the art of printing. And it is worth mention in passing that, as an example of fine typography, the earliest book printed with movable types, the Gutenberg, or "forty-two line Bible" of about 1455, has never been surpassed.

Printing, then, for our purpose, may be considered as the art of making books by means of movable types. Now, as all books not primarily intended as picture-books consist principally of types composed to form letterpress, it is of the first importance that the letter used should be fine in form; especially as no more time is occupied, or cost incurred, in casting, setting, or printing beautiful letters than in the same operations with ugly ones. And it was a matter of course that in the Middle Ages, when the craftsmen took care that beautiful form should always be a part of their productions whatever they were, the forms of printed letters should be beautiful, and that their arrangement on the page should be reasonable and a help to the shapeliness of the letters themselves. The Middle Ages brought caligraphy to perfection, and it was natural therefore that the forms of printed letters should follow more or less closely those of the written character, and they followed them very closely. The first books were printed in black letter, *i.e.* the letter which was a Gothic development of the ancient Roman character, and which developed more completely and satisfactorily on the side of the "lower-case" than the capital letters; the "lower-case" being in fact invented in the *early* Middle Ages. The earliest book printed with movable type, the aforesaid Gutenberg Bible, is printed in letters which are an exact

Printing.

Printing. imitation of the more formal ecclesiastical writing which obtained at that time; this has since been called "missal type," and was in fact the kind of letter used in the many splendid missals, psalters, etc., produced by printing in the fifteenth century. But the first Bible actually dated (which also was printed at Maintz by Peter Schœffer in the year 1462) imitates a much freer hand, simpler, rounder, and less *spiky*, and therefore far pleasanter and easier to read. On the whole the type of this book may be considered the *ne-plus-ultra* of Gothic type, especially as regards the lower-case letters; and type very similar was used during the next fifteen or twenty years not only by Schœffer, but by printers in Strasburg, Basle, Paris, Lubeck, and other cities. But though on the whole, except in Italy, Gothic letter was most often used, a very few years saw the birth of Roman character not only in Italy, but in Germany and France. In 1465 Sweynheim and Pannartz began printing in the monastery of Subiaco near Rome, and used an exceedingly beautiful type, which is indeed to look at a transition between Gothic and Roman, but which must certainly have come from the study of the twelfth or even the eleventh century MSS. They printed very few books in this type, three only; but in their very first books in Rome, beginning with the year 1468, they discarded this for a more completely Roman and far less beautiful letter. But about the same year Mentelin at Strasburg began to print in a type which is distinctly Roman; and the next year Gunther Zeiner at Augsburg followed suit; while in 1470 at Paris Udalric Gering and his associates turned out the first books printed in France, also in Roman

Printing. character. The Roman type of all these printers is similar in character, and is very simple and legible, and unaffectedly designed for *use;* but it is by no means without beauty. It must be said that it is in no way like the transition type of Subiaco, and though more Roman than that, yet scarcely more like the complete Roman type of the earliest printers of Rome.

A further development of the Roman letter took place at Venice. John of Spires and his brother Vindelin, followed by Nicholas Jenson, began to print in that city, 1469, 1470; their type is on the lines of the German and French rather than of the Roman printers. Of Jenson it must be said that he carried the development of Roman type as far as it can go: his letter is admirably clear and regular, but at least as beautiful as any other Roman type. After his death in the "fourteen eighties," or at least by 1490, printing in Venice had declined very much; and though the famous family of Aldus restored its technical excellence, rejecting battered letters, and paying great attention to the "press work" or actual process of *printing*, yet their type is artistically on a much lower level than Jenson's, and in fact they must be considered to have ended the age of fine printing in Italy. Printing.

Jenson, however, had many contemporaries who used beautiful type, some of which—as, *e.g.*, that of Jacobus Rubeus or Jacques le Rouge—is scarcely distinguishable from his. It was these great Venetian printers, together with their brethren of Rome, Milan, Parma, and one or two other cities, who produced the splendid editions of the Classics, which are one of the great glories of the printer's art, and are

Printing. worthy representatives of the eager enthusiasm for the revived learning of that epoch. By far the greater part of these *Italian* printers, it should be mentioned, were Germans or Frenchmen, working under the influence of Italian opinion and aims.

It must be understood that through the whole of the fifteenth and the first quarter of the sixteenth centuries the Roman letter was used side by side with the Gothic. Even in Italy most of the theological and law books were printed in Gothic letter, which was generally more formally Gothic than the printing of the German workmen, many of whose types, indeed, like that of the Subiaco works, are of a transitional character. This was notably the case with the early works printed at Ulm, and in a somewhat lesser degree at Augsburg. In fact Gunther Zeiner's first type (afterwards used by Schussler) is remarkably like the type of the before-mentioned Subiaco books.

In the Low Countries and Cologne, which were very fertile of printed books, Gothic was the favourite. The characteristic Dutch type, as represented by the excellent printer Gerard Leew, is very pronounced and uncompromising Gothic. This type was introduced into England by Wynkyn de Worde, Caxton's successor, and was used there with very little variation all through the sixteenth and seventeenth centuries, and indeed into the eighteenth. Most of Caxton's own types are of an earlier character, though they also much resemble Flemish or Cologne letter. After the end of the fifteenth century the degradation of printing, especially in Germany and Italy, went on apace; and by the end of the sixteenth century there was no

Printing. really beautiful printing done: the best, mostly French or Low-Country, was neat and clear, but without any *distinction*; the worst, which perhaps was the English, was a terrible falling-off from the work of the earlier presses; and things got worse and worse through the whole of the seventeenth century, so that in the eighteenth printing was very miserably performed. In England about this time, an attempt was made (notably by Caslon, who started business in London as a type-founder in 1720) to improve the letter in form. Caslon's type is clear and neat, and fairly well designed; he seems to have taken the letter of the Elzevirs of the seventeenth century for his model: type cast from his matrices is still in everyday use.

In spite, however, of his praiseworthy efforts, printing had still one last degradation to undergo. The seventeenth century founts were bad rather negatively than positively. But for the beauty of the earlier work they might have seemed tolerable. It was reserved for the founders of the later eighteenth century to produce letters which are *positively* ugly, and which, it may be added, are dazzling and unpleasant to the eye owing to the clumsy thickening and vulgar thinning of the lines: for the seventeenth-century letters are at least pure and simple in line. The Italian, Bodoni, and the Frenchman, Didot, were the leaders in this luckless change, though our own Baskerville, who was at work some years before them, went much on the same lines; but his letters, though uninteresting and poor, are not nearly so gross and vulgar as those of either the Italian or the Frenchman.

With this change the art of printing

Printing. touched bottom, so far as fine printing is concerned, though paper did not get to its worst till about 1840. The Chiswick press in 1844 revived Caslon's founts, printing for Messrs. Longman the Diary of Lady Willoughby. This experiment was so far successful that about 1850 Messrs. Miller and Richard of Edinburgh were induced to cut punches for a series of "old style" letters. These and similar founts, cast by the above firm and others, have now come into general use and are obviously a great improvement on the ordinary "modern style" in use in England, which is in fact the Bodoni type a little reduced in ugliness. The design of the letters of this modern "old style" leaves a good deal to be desired, and the whole effect is a little too gray, owing to the thinness of the letters. It must be remembered, however, that most modern printing is done by machinery on soft paper, and not by the hand press, and these somewhat wiry letters are suitable for the machine process, which would not do justice to letters of more generous design.

It is discouraging to note that the improvement of the last fifty years is almost wholly confined to Great Britain. Here and there a book is printed in France or Germany with some pretension to good taste, but the general revival of the old forms has made no way in those countries. Italy is contentedly stagnant. America has produced a good many showy books, the typography, paper, and illustrations of which are, however, all wrong, oddity rather than rational beauty and meaning being apparently the thing sought for both in the letters and the illustrations.

To say a few words on the principles

Printing. of design in typography: it is obvious that legibility is the first thing to be aimed at in the forms of the letters; this is best furthered by the avoidance of irrational swellings and spiky projections, and by the using of careful purity of line. Even the Caslon type when enlarged shows great shortcomings in this respect: the ends of many of the letters such as the t and e are hooked up in a vulgar and meaningless way, instead of ending in the sharp and clear stroke of Jenson's letters; there is a grossness in the upper finishings of letters like the c, the a, and so on, an ugly pear-shaped swelling defacing the form of the letter: in short, it happens to this craft, as to others, that the utilitarian practice, though it professes to avoid ornament, still clings to a foolish, because misunderstood conventionality, deduced from what was once ornament, and is by no means *useful*; which title can only be claimed by *artistic* practice, whether the art in it be conscious or unconscious.

Printing.

In no characters is the contrast between the ugly and vulgar illegibility of the modern type and the elegance and legibility of the ancient more striking than in the Arabic numerals. In the old print each figure has its definite individuality, and one cannot be mistaken for the other; in reading the modern figures the eyes must be strained before the reader can have any reasonable assurance that he has a 5, an 8, or a 3 before him, unless the press work is of the best: this is awkward if you have to read Bradshaw's Guide in a hurry.

One of the differences between the fine type and the utilitarian must probably be put down to a misapprehension of a commercial necessity: this is the

Printing. narrowing of the modern letters. Most of Jenson's letters are designed within a square, the modern letters are narrowed by a third or thereabout; but while this gain of space very much hampers the possibility of beauty of design, it is not a real gain, for the modern printer throws the gain away by putting inordinately wide spaces between his lines, which, probably, the lateral compression of his letters renders necessary. Commercialism again compels the use of type too small in size to be comfortable reading: the size known as "Long primer" ought to be the smallest size used in a book meant to be read. Here, again, if the practice of "leading" were retrenched larger type could be used without enhancing the price of a book.

One very important matter in "setting up" for fine printing is the "spacing," that is, the lateral distance

Printing.

of words from one another. In good printing the spaces between the words should be as near as possible equal (it is impossible that they should be quite equal except in lines of poetry) ; modern printers understand this, but it is only practised in the very best establishments. But another point which they should attend to they almost always disregard ; this is the tendency to the formation of ugly meandering white lines or "rivers" in the page, a blemish which can be nearly, though not wholly, avoided by care and forethought, the desirable thing being "the breaking of the line" as in bonding masonry or brickwork, thus : The general *solidity* of a page is much to be sought for : modern printers generally overdo the "whites" in the spacing, a defect probably forced on them by the characterless quality of the letters.

Printing. For where these are boldly and carefully designed, and each letter is thoroughly individual in form, the words may be set much closer together, without loss of clearness. No definite rules, however, except the avoidance of "rivers" and excess of white, can be given for the spacing, which requires the constant exercise of judgment and taste on the part of the printer.

The position of the page on the paper should be considered if the book is to have a satisfactory look. Here once more the almost invariable modern practice is in opposition to a natural sense of proportion. From the time when books first took their present shape till the end of the sixteenth century, or indeed later, the page so lay on the paper that there was more space allowed to the bottom and fore margin than to the top and back of the paper, thus : Printing.

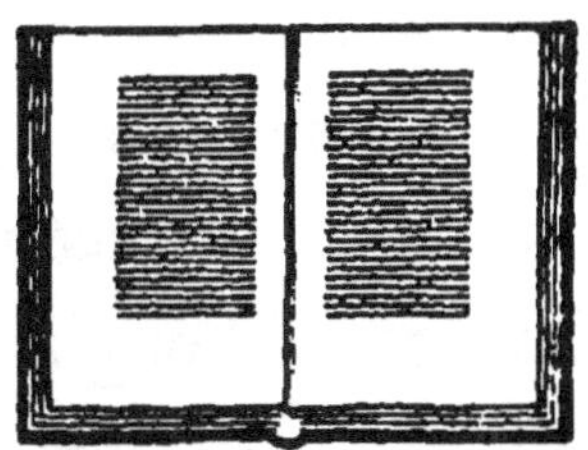

the unit of the book being looked on as the two pages forming an opening. The modern printer, in the teeth of the evidence given by his own eyes, considers the single page as the unit, and prints the page in the middle of his paper—only nominally so, however, in many cases, since when he uses a headline he counts that in, the result as measured by the eye being that the lower margin is less than the top one, and that the whole opening has an upside-down look vertically, and that laterally the page looks as if it were being driven off the paper.

Printing. The paper on which the printing is to be done is a necessary part of our subject: of this it may be said that though there is some good paper made now, it is never used except for very expensive books, although it would not materially increase the cost in all but the very cheapest. The paper that is used for ordinary books is exceedingly bad even in this country, but is beaten in the race for vileness by that made in America, which is the worst conceivable. There seems to be no reason why ordinary paper should not be better made, even allowing the necessity for a very low price; but any improvement must be based on showing openly that the cheap article *is* cheap, *e.g.* the cheap paper should not sacrifice toughness and durability to a smooth and white surface, which should be indications of a delicacy of material and manufacture which would of necessity increase its cost. One fruitful source of badness in paper is the habit that publishers have of eking out a thin volume by printing it on thick paper almost of the substance of cardboard, a device which deceives nobody, and makes a book very unpleasant to read. On the whole, a small book should be printed on paper which is as thin as may be without being transparent. The paper used for printing the small highly ornamented French service-books about the beginning of the sixteenth century is a model in this respect, being thin, tough, and opaque. However, the fact must not be blinked that machine-made paper cannot in the nature of things be made of so good a texture as that made by hand.

The ornamentation of printed books is too wide a subject to be dealt with fully here; but one thing must be said on it. The essential point to be remembered is that the ornament, whatever it is, whether picture or pattern-work, should form *part of the page*, should be a part of the whole scheme of the book. Simple as this proposition is, it is necessary to be stated, because the modern practice is to disregard the relation between the printing and the ornament altogether, so that if the two are helpful to one another it is a mere matter of accident. The due relation of letter to pictures and other ornament was thoroughly understood by the old printers; so that even when the woodcuts are very rude indeed, the proportions of the page still give pleasure by the sense of richness that the cuts and letter together convey. When, as is most often the case, there is actual beauty in the cuts, the books so ornamented are amongst the most delightful works of art that have ever been produced. Therefore, granted well-designed type, due spacing of the lines and words, and proper position of the page on the paper, all books might be at least comely and well-looking : and if to these good qualities were added really beautiful ornament and pictures, printed books might once again illustrate to the full the position of our Society that a work of utility might be also a work of art, if we cared to make it so.

WILLIAM MORRIS.
EMERY WALKER.

BOOKBINDING

MODERN bookbinding dates from the application of printing to literature, and in essentials has remained unchanged to the present day, though in those outward characteristics, which appeal to the touch and to the eye, and constitute binding in an artistic sense, it has gone through many changes for better and for worse, which, in the opinion of the writer, have resulted, in the main, in the exaggeration of technical skill and in the death of artistic fancy.

The first operation of the modern

binder is to fold or refold the printed sheet into a section, and to gather the sections, numbered or lettered at the foot, in their proper order into a volume.

Book-binding.

The sections are then taken, one by one, placed face downwards in a frame, and sewn through the back by a continuous thread running backwards and forwards along the backs of the sections to upright strings fastened at regular intervals in the sewing frame. This process unites the sections to one another in series one after the other, and permits the perusal of the book by the simple turning of leaf after leaf upon the hinge formed by the thread and the back of the section.

A volume, or series of sections, so treated, the ends of the string being properly secured, is essentially "bound"; all that is subsequently done is done for the protection or for the decoration of the volume or of its cover.

The sides of a volume are protected by millboards, called shortly "boards." The boards themselves and the back are protected by a cover of leather, vellum, silk, linen, or paper, wholly or in part. The edges of the volume are protected by the projection of the boards beyond them at top, bottom, and fore-edge, and usually by being cut smooth and gilt.

A volume so bound and protected may be decorated by tooling or otherwise upon all the exposed surfaces (upon the edges, the sides, and the back) and may be designated by lettering upon the back or the sides.

The degree in which a bound book is protected and decorated will determine the class to which the binding will belong.

(1) In *cloth binding*, the cover, called a "case," is made apart from the book, and is attached as a whole after the book is sewn.

Book-binding.

(2) In *half binding*, the cover is built up for and on each individual book, but the boards of which it is composed are only partly covered with the leather or other material which covers the back.

(3) In *whole binding*, the boards are wholly covered with leather or other durable material, which in half binding covers only a portion of them.

(4) In *extra binding*, whole binding is advanced a stage higher by decoration. Of course in the various stages the details vary commensurately with the stage itself, being more or less elaborate as the stage is higher or lower in the scale.

The process of *extra binding* set out in more detail is as follows:—

Book-binding.

(1) First the sections are folded or refolded.

(2) Then "end-papers"—sections of plain paper added at the beginning and end of the volume to protect the first and last, the most exposed, sections of printed matter constituting the volume proper—having been prepared and added, the sections are beaten, or rolled, or pressed, to make them "solid."

The end-papers are usually added at a later stage, and are pasted on, and not sewn, but, in the opinion of the writer, it is better to add them at this stage, and to sew them and not to paste them.

(3) Then the sections are sewn as already described.

(4) When sewn the volume passes into the hands of the "forwarder," who

(5) "Makes" the back, beating it round, if the back is to be round, and "backing" it, or making it fan out from

the centre to right and left and project at the edges, to form a kind of ridge to receive and to protect the edges of the boards which form the sides of the cover.

(6) The back having been made, the "boards" (made of millboard, and originally of wood) for the protection of the sides are made and cut to shape, and attached by lacing into them the ends of the strings upon which the book has been sewn.

(7) The boards having been attached, the edges of the book are now cut smooth and even at the top, bottom, and fore-edge, the edges of the boards being used as guides for the purpose. In some cases the order is reversed, and the edges are first cut and then the boards.

(8) The edges may now be coloured and gilt, and if it is proposed to "gauffer" or to decorate them with tooling, they are so treated at this stage.

Book-binding.

(9) The head-band is next worked on at head and tail, and the back lined with paper or leather or other material to keep the head-band in its place and to strengthen the back itself.

The book is now ready to be covered.

(10) If the book is covered with leather, the leather is carefully pared all round the edges and along the line of the back, to make the edges sharp and the joints free.

(11) The book having been covered, the depression on the inside of the boards caused by the overlap of the leather is filled in with paper, so that the entire inner surface may be smooth and even, and ready to receive the first and last leaves of the end-papers, which finally are cut to shape and pasted down, leaving the borders only uncovered.

Sometimes, however, the first and last leaves of the "end-papers" are of silk,

Book-binding.

and the "joint" of leather, in which case, of course, the end-papers are not pasted down, but the insides of the boards are independently treated, and are covered, sometimes with leather, sometimes with silk or other material.

The book is now "forwarded," and passes into the hands of the "finisher" to be tooled or decorated, or "finished" as it is called.

The decoration in gold on the surface of leather is wrought out, bit by bit, by means of small brass stamps called "tools."

The steps of the process are shortly as follows :—

(12) The pattern having been settled and worked out on paper, it is "transferred" to, or marked out on, the various surfaces to which it is to be applied.

Each surface is then prepared in

succession, and, if large, bit by bit, to receive the gold.

(13) First the leather is washed with water or with vinegar.

(14) Then the pattern is pencilled over with "glaire" (white of egg beaten up and drained off), or the surface is wholly washed with it.

(15) Next it is smeared lightly with grease or oil.

(16) And, finally, the gold (gold leaf) is applied by a pad of cotton wool, or a flat thin brush called a "tip."

(17) The pattern, visible through the gold, is now reimpressed or worked with the tools heated to about the temperature of boiling water, and the unimpressed or waste gold is removed by an oiled rag, leaving the pattern in gold and the rest of the leather clear.

These several operations are, in

England, usually distributed among five classes of persons.

(1) The *superintendent* or person responsible for the whole work.

(2) The *sewer*, usually a woman, who folds, sews, and makes the head-bands.

(3) The *book-edge gilder*, who gilds the edges. Usually a craft apart.

(4) The *forwarder*, who performs all the other operations leading up to the finishing.

(5) The *finisher*, who decorates and letters the volume after it is forwarded.

In Paris the work is still further distributed, a special workman (*couvreur*) being employed to prepare the leather for covering and to cover.

In the opinion of the writer, the work, as a craft of beauty, suffers, as do the workmen, from the allocation of different operations to different workmen. The work should be conceived of as one, and be wholly executed by one person, or at most by two, and especially should there be no distinction between "finisher" and "forwarder," between "executant" and "artist."

The following technical names may serve to call attention to the principal features of a bound book.

(1) The *back*, the posterior edge of the volume upon which at the present time the title is usually placed. Formerly it was placed on the fore-edge or side.

The back may be (*a*) convex or concave or flat; (*b*) marked horizontally with bands, or smooth from head to tail; (*c*) tight, the leather or other covering adhering to the back itself, or hollow, the leather or other covering not so adhering; and (*d*) stiff or flexible.

(2) *Edges*, the three other edges of

the book,—the top, the bottom, and the fore-edge.

(3) *Bands*, the cords upon which the book is sewn, and which, if not "let in" or embedded in the back, appear on it as parallel ridges. The ridges are, however, usually artificial, the real bands being "let in" to facilitate the sewing, and their places supplied by thin slips of leather cut to resemble them and glued on the back. This process also enables the forwarder to give great sharpness and finish to this part of his work, if he think it worth while.

(4) *Between-bands*, the space between the bands.

(5) *Head* and *tail*, the top and bottom of the back.

(6) The *head-band* and *head-cap*, the fillet of silk worked in buttonhole stitch at the head and tail, and the cap or cover of leather over it. The head-

band had its origin probably in the desire to strengthen the back and to resist the strain when a book is pulled by head or tail from the shelf.

(7) *Boards*, the sides of the cover, stiff or limp, thick or thin, in all degrees.

(8) *Squares*, the projection of the boards beyond the edges of the book. These may be shallow or deep in all degrees, limited only by the purpose they have to fulfil and the danger they will themselves be exposed to if too deep.

(9) *Borders*, the overlaps of leather on the insides of the boards.

(10) *Proof*, the rough edges of leaves left uncut in cutting the edges to show where the original margin was, and to prove that the cutting has not been too severe.

Book-binding.

The life of bookbinding is in the dainty mutation of its mutable elements—back, bands, boards, squares, decoration. These elements admit of almost endless variation, singly and in combination, in kind and in degree. In fact, however, they are now almost always uniformly treated or worked up to one type or set of types. This is the death of bookbinding as a craft of beauty.

The finish, moreover, or execution, has outrun invention, and is the great characteristic of modern bookbinding. This again, the inversion of the due order, is, in the opinion of the writer, but as the carving on the tomb of a dead art, and itself dead.

A well-bound beautiful book is neither of one type, nor finished so that its highest praise is that "had it been made by a machine it could not have been made better." It is individual; it

Book-binding.

is instinct with the hand of him who made it; it is pleasant to feel, to handle, and to see; it is the original work of an original mind working in freedom simultaneously with hand and heart and brain to produce a thing of use, which all time shall agree ever more and more also to call "a thing of beauty."

T. J. COBDEN-SANDERSON.

OF MURAL PAINTING

THERE seems no precise reason why the subject of this note should differ much from that of Mr. Crane's article on "Decorative Painting" (pp. 39-51). "Mural Painting" need not, as such, consist of any one sort of painting more than another. "Decorative Painting" does seem, on the other hand, to indicate a certain desire or undertaking to render the object painted more pleasant to the beholder's eye.

From long habit, however, chiefly induced by the constant practice of the Italians of modern times, "Mural

Painting" has come to be looked upon as figure painting (in fact, the human figure exclusively) on walls—and no other sort of objects can sufficiently impart that dignity to a building which it seems to crave for. I can think of no valid reason why a set of rooms, or walls, should not be decorated with animals in lieu of "humans," as the late Mr. Trelawney used to call us: one wall to be devoted to monkeys, a second to be filled in with tigers, a third to be given up to horses, etc. etc. I know men in England, and, I believe, some artists, who would be delighted with the substitution. But I hope the general sense of the public would be set against such subjects, and the lowering effects of them on every one, and the kind of humiliation we should feel at knowing them to exist.

I have been informed that in Berlin

the walls of the rooms where the antique statues are kept have been painted with mixed subjects representing antique buildings with antique Greek views and landscapes, to back up, as it were, the statues. I must own it, that without having seen the decoration in question, I feel filled with extreme aversion for the plan. The more so when one considers the extreme unlikelihood of the same being made tolerable in colour at Berlin. I have also been told that some painters in the North of England, bitten with a desire to decorate buildings, have painted one set of rooms with landscapes. This, without the least knowledge of the works in question, as landscapes, I must allow I regret. There is, it seems to me, an unbridgeable chasm, not to be passed, between landscape art and the decoration of walls; for the very essence of the landscape art is distance, whereas the very essence of the wall-picture is its solidity, or, at least, its not appearing to be a hole in the wall. On the matter of subjects fit for painting on walls I may have a few words to say farther on in this paper, but first I had better set down what little I have to advise with regard to the material and mode of executing.

The old-fashioned Italian or "Buon Fresco" I look upon as practically given up in this country, and every other European country that has not a climate to equal Italy. If the climate of Paris will not admit of this process, how much less is our damp, foggy, changeable atmosphere likely to put up with it for many years! It is true that the frescoes of William Dyce have lasted for some thirty years without apparent damage; but also it is the case that the Queen's Robing Rooms in the House of Lords have been specially guarded against atmospheric changes of temperature. Next to real fresco, there has been in repute for a time the waterglass process, in which Daniel Maclise's great paintings have been executed. I see no precise reason why these noble works should not last, and defy climate for many, many long years yet; though from want of experience he very much endangered this durability through the too lavish application of the medium. But in Germany, the country of waterglass, the process is already in bad repute. The third alternative, "spirit fresco," or what we in England claim as the Gambier-Parry process, has, I understand, superseded it. I have myself painted in this system seven works on the walls of the Manchester Town Hall, and have had no reason to complain of their behaviour. Since beginning the series, however, a fresh change has come over the fortunes of mural art in the fact that, in France (what most strongly recommends itself to common sense), the mural painters have now taken to painting on canvas, which is afterwards cemented, or what the French call "maronflée," on to the wall. White-lead and oil, with a very small admixture of rosin melted in oil, are the ingredients used. It is laid on cold and plentifully on the wall and on the back of the picture, and the painting pressed down with a cloth or handkerchief: nothing further being required, saving to guard the edges of the canvas from curling up before the white-lead has had time to harden. The advantage of this process of cementing lies in the fact that with each succeeding year it must become harder and more like stone in its consistency. The canvases may be prepared as if for oil painting, and painted with common oil-colours flatted (or matted) afterwards by gum-elemi and spike-oil. Or the canvas may be prepared with the Gambier-Parry colour and painted in that very *mat* medium. The canvases should if possible be fine in texture, as better adapted for adhering to the wall. The advantage of this process is that, should at any time, through neglect, damp invade the wall, and the canvas show a tendency to get loose, it would be easy to replace it; or the canvas might be altogether detached from the wall and strained as a picture.

I must now return to the choice of subject, a matter of much importance, but on which it is difficult to give advice. One thing, however, may be urged as a rule, and that is, that very dark or Rembrandtesque subjects are particularly unsuited for mural paintings. I cannot go into the reasons for this, but a slight experiment ought to satisfy the painter, having once heard the principle enunciated : that is, if he belong to the class likely to succeed at such work.

Another *sine qua non* as to subject is that the painter himself must be allowed to select it. It is true that certain limitations may be accorded—for instance, the artist may be required to select a subject with certain tendencies in it—but the actual invention of the subject and working out of it must be his. In fact, the painter himself is the only judge of what he is likely to carry out well and of the subjects that are paintable. Then much depends on whom the works are for; if for the general public, and carried out with their money, care (it seems to me but fair) should be taken that the subjects are such as they can understand and take interest in. If, on the contrary, you are painting for highly-cultured people with a turn for Greek myths, it is quite another thing; then, such a subject as "Eros reproaching his brother Anteros for his coldness" might be one offering opportunities for shades of sentiment suited to the givers of the commissions concerned. But for such as have not been trained to entertain these refinements, downright facts, either in history or in sociology, are calculated most to excite the imagination. It is not always necessary for the spectator to be exact in his conclusions. I remember once at Manchester, the members of a Young Men's Christian Association had come to a meeting in the great hall. Some of them were there too soon, and so were looking round the room. One observed: "What's this about?" His friend answered: "Fallen off a ladder, the police are running him in!" Well, this was not quite correct. A wounded young Danish chieftain was being hurried out of Manchester on his comrade's shoulders, with a view to save his life. The Phrygian helmets of the Danes indicated neither firemen nor policemen; but the idea was one of misfortune, and care bestowed on it—and did as well, and showed sympathy in a somewhat uncultivated, though well-intentioned, class of Lancastrians. On the other hand, I have noticed that subjects that interest infallibly all classes, educated or illiterate, are religious subjects. It is not a question of piety—but comes from the simple breadth of poetry and humanity usually involved in this class of subject. That the amount of religiosity in either spectator or producer has nothing to do with the feeling is clear if we consider.

The Spaniards are one of the most

religious peoples ever known, and yet their art is singularly deficient in this quality. Were there ever two great painters as wanting in the sacred feeling as Velasquez and Murillo? and yet, in all probability, they were more religious than ourselves.

It only remains for me to point to the fact that mural painting, when it has been practised jointly by those who were at the same time easel-painters, has invariably raised those painters to far higher flights and instances of style than they seem capable of in the smaller path. Take the examples left us, say by Raphael and Michel Angelo, or some of the earlier masters, such as the "Fulminati" of Signorelli, compared with his specimens in our National Gallery; or the works left on walls by even less favoured artists, such as Domenichino and Andrea del Sarto, or the French de la Roche's

"Hémicycle," or our own great painters Dyce and Maclise's frescoes; the same rise in style, the same improvement, is everywhere to be noticed, both in drawing, in colour, and in flesh-painting.

F. Madox Brown.

OF SGRAFFITO WORK

THE Italian words Graffiato, Sgraffiato, or Sgraffito, mean "Scratched," and scratched work is the oldest form of graphic expression and surface decoration used by man.

The term Sgraffito is, however, specially used to denote decoration scratched or incised upon plaster or potter's clay while still soft, and for beauty of effect depends either solely upon lines thus incised according to design, with the resulting contrast of surfaces, or partly upon such lines and contrast, and partly upon an under-coat of colour revealed by the incisions; while, again, the means at disposal may be increased by varying the colours of the under-coat in accordance with the design.

Of the potter's sgraffito I have no experience, but it is my present purpose briefly and practically to examine the method, special aptitudes, and limitations of polychrome sgraffito as applied to the plasterer's craft.

First, then, as to method. Given the wall intended to be treated: granted the completion of the scheme of decoration, the cartoons having been executed in several colours and the outlines firmly pricked, and further, all things being ready for beginning work. Hack off any existing plaster from the wall: when bare, rake and sweep out the joints thoroughly: when clean, give the wall as much water as it will drink: lay the coarse coat, leaving the face rough in order to make a good key for the next coat: when sufficiently set, fix your cartoon in its destined position with slate nails: pounce through the pricked outlines: remove the cartoon: replace the nails in the register holes: mark in with a brush in white oil paint the spaces for the different colours as shown in the cartoon, and pounced in outline on the coarse coat, placing the letters B, R, Y, etc., as the case may be, in order to show the plasterer where to lay the different colours—Black, Red, Yellow, etc.: give the wall as much water as it will drink: lay the colour coat in accordance with the lettered spaces on the coarse coat, taking care not to displace the register nails, and leaving plenty of key for the final surface coat.

Of Sgraffito Work.

In laying the colour coat, calculate how much of the colour surface it may be advisable to get on the wall, as the same duration of time should be maintained throughout the work between the laying of the colour coat and the following on with the final surface coat—for this reason, if the colour coat sets hard before the final coat is laid, it will not be possible to scrape up the colour to its full strength wherever it may be revealed by incision of the design. When sufficiently set, *i.e.* in about 24 hours, follow on with the final surface coat, only laying as much as can be cut and cleaned up in a day: when this is sufficiently steady, fix up the cartoon in its registered position : pounce through the pricked outlines : remove the cartoon and cut the design in the surface coat before it sets : then, if your register is correct, you will cut through to different colours according to the design, and in the course of a few days the work should set as hard and homogeneous as stone, and as damp-proof as the nature of things permits.

The three coats above referred to may be gauged as follows :—

Coarse Coat.—2 or 3 of sharp clean sand to 1 of Portland, to be laid about $\frac{3}{4}$ inch in thickness. This coat is to promote an even suction and to keep back damp.

Colour Coat.—1 of colour to 1$\frac{1}{2}$ of old Portland, to be laid about $\frac{1}{8}$ inch in thickness. Specially prepared distemper colours should be used, and amongst such may be mentioned golden ochre, Turkey red, Indian red, manganese black, lime blue, and umber.

Final Surface Coat.—Aberthaw lime and selenitic cement, both sifted through a fine sieve—the proportions of the gauge depend upon the heat of the lime: or, Parian cement sifted as above—air-slaked for 24 hours, and gauged with water coloured with ochre, so as to give a creamy tone when the plaster dries out: or, 3 of selenitic cement to 2 of silver sand, both sifted as above—this may be used for out-door work.

Individual taste and experience must decide as to the thickness of the final coat, but if laid between $\frac{1}{8}$ and $\frac{1}{12}$ inch, and the lines cut with slanting edges, a side light gives emphasis to the finished result, making the outlines tell alternately as they take the light or cast a shadow. Plasterers' small tools of various kinds and knife-blades fixed in tool handles will be found suited to the simple craft of cutting and clearing off the final surface coat; but as to this a craftsman finds his own tools by experience, and indeed by the same acquired perception must be interpreted all the foregoing directions, and specially that ambiguous word, dear to the writers of recipes,—*Sufficient.*

Thus far method. Now, as to special aptitudes and limitations. Sgraffito work may claim a special aptitude for design whose centre of aim is line. It has no beauty of material like glass, no mystery of surface like mosaic, no pre-eminence of subtly-woven tone and colour like tapestry; yet it gives freer play to line than any of these mentioned fields of design, and a cartoon for sgraffito can be executed in facsimile, undeviated by warp and woof, and unchecked by angular tesseræ or lead lines. True, hardness of design may easily result from this aptitude, indeed is to a certain extent inherent to the method under examination, but in overcoming this danger and in making the most of this aptitude is the artist discovered.

Sgraffito from its very nature "asserts

the wall"; that is, preserves the solid appearance of the building which it is intended to decorate. The decoration is in the wall rather than on the wall. It seems to be organic. The inner surface of the actual wall changes colour in puzzling but orderly sequence, as the upper surface passes into expressive lines and spaces, delivers its simple message, and then relapses into silence; but whether incised with intricate design, or left in plain relieving spaces, the wall receives no further treatment, the marks of float, trowel, and scraper remain, and combine to make a natural surface.

It compels the work to be executed *in situ*. The studio must be exchanged for the scaffold, and the result should justify the inconvenience. However carefully the scheme of decoration may be designed, slight yet important modifications and readjustments will probably be found necessary in the transfer from cartoon to wall; and though the ascent of the scaffold may seem an indignity to those who prefer to suffer vicariously in the execution of their works, and though we of the nineteenth know, as Cennini of the fifteenth century knew, "that painting pictures is the proper employment of a gentleman, and with velvet on his back he may paint what he pleases," still the fact remains, that if decoration is to attain that inevitable fitness for its place which is the fulfilment of design, this "proper employment of a gentleman" must be postponed, and velvet exchanged for blouse.

It compels a quick, sure manner of work; and this quickness of execution, due to the setting nature of the final coat, and to the consequent necessity of working against time, gives an appearance of strenuous ease to the firm incisions

Of Sgraffito Work.

and spaces by which the design is expressed, and a living energy of line to the whole. Again, the setting nature of the colour coat suggests, and naturally lends itself to, an occasional addition in the shape of mosaic to the means at disposal, and a little glitter here and there will be found to go a long way in giving points of emphasis and play to large surfaces.

It compels the artist to adopt a limited colour scheme—a limitation, and yet one which may almost be welcomed as an aptitude, for of colours in decorative work multiplication may be said to be a vexation.

Finally, the limitations of sgraffito as a method of expression are the same as those of all incised or line work. By it you can express ideas and suggest life, but you cannot realise,—cannot imitate the natural objects on which your graphic language is founded. The means at disposal are too scanty. Item: white lines and spaces relieved against and slightly raised on a coloured ground; coloured lines and spaces slightly sunk on a white surface; intricacy relieved by simplicity of line, and again either relieved by plain spaces of coloured ground or white surface. Indeed they are simple means. Yet line still remains the readiest manner of graphic expression; and if in the strength of limitation our past masters of the arts and crafts have had power to "free, arouse, dilate" by their simple record of hand and soul, we also should be able to bring forth new achievement from old method, and to suggest the life and express the ideas which sway the latter years of our own century.

HEYWOOD SUMNER.

OF STUCCO AND GESSO

FEW things are more disheartening to the pursuer of plastic art than finding that, when he has carried his own labour to a certain point, he has to entrust it to another in order to render it permanent and useful. If he models in clay and wishes it burnt into terra cotta, the shrinkage and risk in firing, and the danger in transport to the kiln, are a nightmare to him. If he wishes it cast in plaster, the distortion by waste-moulding, or the cost of piece-moulding, are serious grievances to him, considering that after all he has but a friable result ; and though this latter objection is minimised by Mrs. Laxton Clark's ingenious process of indurating plaster, yet I am persuaded that most modellers would prefer to complete their work in some permanent form with their own hands.

Of Stucco and Gesso.

Having this desirable end in view, I wish to draw their attention to some disused processes which once largely prevailed, by which the artist is enabled to finish, and render durable and vendible, his work, without having to part with it or pay for another's aid.

These old processes are modelling in Stucco-duro and Gesso.

Stucco-duro, although of very ancient practice, is now practically a lost art. The materials required are simply well-burnt and slacked lime, a little fine sand, and some finely-ground unburnt limestone or white marble dust. These are well tempered together with water and beaten up with sticks until a good workable paste results. In fact, the preparation of the materials is exactly the same as that described by Vitruvius, who recommends that the fragments of marble be sifted into three degrees of fineness, using the coarser for the rough bossage, the medium for the general modelling, and the finest for the surface finish, after which it can be polished with chalk and powdered lime if necessary. Indeed, to so fine a surface can this material be brought, and so highly can it be polished, that he mentions its use for mirrors.

The only caution that it is needful to give is to avoid working too quickly; for, as Sir Henry Wooton, King James's ambassador at Venice, who greatly advocated the use of stucco-duro, observed, the stucco worker "makes his figures by addition and the carver by subtraction," and to avoid too great risk of the work cracking in drying, these additions must be made slowly where the relief is great. If the relief is very great, or if a figure of large dimensions is essayed, it may be needful even to delay the drying of the stucco, and the addition of a little stiff paste will insure this, so that the work may be consecutively worked upon for many days.

From the remains of the stucco work of classic times left us, we can realise how perfectly workable this material was; and if you examine the plaster casts taken from some most delicate low-relief plaques in stucco exhumed some ten years ago near the Villa Farnesina at Rome, or the rougher and readier fragments of stucco-duro itself from some Italo-Greek tombs, both of which are to be seen in the South Kensington Museum, you will at once be convinced of the great applicability of the process.

Of Stucco and Gesso.

With the decadence of classic art some portion of the process seems to have been lost, and the use of pounded travertine was substituted for white marble; but, as the *bassi-relievi* of the early Renaissance were mostly decorated with colour, this was not important. The ground colours seem generally to have been laid on whilst the stucco was wet, as in fresco, and the details heightened with tempera or encaustic colours, sometimes with accessories enriched in gilt "gesso" (of which hereafter). Many remains of these exist, and in the Nineteenth Winter Exhibition of the Royal Academy there were no less than twelve very interesting examples of it exhibited, and in the South Kensington Museum are some few moderately good illustrations of it.

It was not, however, until the sixteenth

century that the old means of producing the highly-finished white stucchi were rediscovered, and this revival of the art as an architectonic accessory is due to the exhumation of the baths of Titus under Leo X. Raphael and Giovanni da Udine were then so struck with the beauty of the stucco work thus exposed to view that its re-use was at once determined upon, and the Loggia of the Vatican was the first result of many experiments, though the re-invented process seems to have been precisely that described by Vitruvius. Naturally, the art of modelling in stucco at once became popular: the patronage of it by the Pope, and the practice of it by the artists who worked for him, gave it the highest sanction, and hardly a building of any architectural importance was erected in Italy during the sixteenth century that did not bear evidence of the artistic craft of the stuccatori.

There has just (Autumn, 1889) arrived at the South Kensington Museum a model of the central hall of the Villa Madama in Rome, thus decorated by Giulio Romano and Giovanni da Udine, which exemplifies the adaptability of the process; and in this model Cav. Mariani has employed stucco-duro for its execution, showing to how high a pitch of finish this material is capable of being carried. Indeed, it was used by goldsmiths for the models for their craft, as being less liable to injury than wax, yet capable of receiving equally delicate treatment; and Benvenuto Cellini modelled the celebrated "button," with "that magnificent big diamond" in the middle, for the cope of Pope Clement, with all its intricate detail, in this material. How minute this work of some six inches diameter was may be inferred from Cellini's own description of it. Above the diamond, in the centre of the piece, was shown God the Father seated, in the act of giving the benediction; below were three children, who, with their arms upraised, were supporting the jewel. One of them, in the middle, was in full relief, the other two in half-relief. "All round I set a crowd of cherubs in divers attitudes. A mantle undulated to the wind around the figure of the Father, from the folds of which cherubs peeped out; and there were many other ornaments besides, which," adds he, and for once we may believe him, "made a very beautiful effect." At the same time, figures larger than life, indeed colossal figures, were executed in it, and in our own country the Italian artists brought over by our Henry VIII. worked in that style for his vanished palace of Nonsuch. Gradually, stucco-duro fell into disuse, and coarse pargetry and modelled plaster ceilings became in later years its sole and degenerate descendants.

Gesso is really a painter's art rather than a sculptor's, and consists in impasto painting with a mixture of plaster of Paris or whiting in glue (the composition with which the ground of his pictures is laid) after roughly modelling the higher forms with tow or some fibrous material incorporated with the gesso ; but it is questionable if gesso is the best vehicle for any but the lowest relief. By it the most subtle and delicate variation of surface can be obtained, and the finest lines pencilled, analogous, in fact, to the fine *pâte sur pâte* work in porcelain. Its chief use in early times was in the accessories of painting, as the nimbi, attributes, and jewellery of the personage represented, and it was almost entirely used as a ground-work for gilding upon. Abundant illustration of this usage will be found in the pictures by the early Italian masters in the National Gallery. The retables of altars were largely decorated in this material, a notable example being that still existing in Westminster Abbey.

Many of the gorgeous accessories to the panoply of war in mediæval times, such as decorative shields and the lighter military accoutrements, were thus ornamented in low relief, and on the high-cruppered and high-peaked saddles it was abundantly displayed. In the sixteenth-century work of Germany it seems to have received an admixture of finely-pounded lithographic stone, or hone stone, by which it became of such hardness as to be taken for sculpture in these materials. Its chief use, however, was for the decoration of the caskets and ornamental objects which make up the refinement of domestic life, and the base representative of it which figures on our picture-frames claims a noble ancestry.

Its tenacity, when well prepared, is exceedingly great, and I have used it on glass, on polished marble, on porcelain, and such like non-absorbent surfaces, from which it can scarcely be separated without destruction of its base. Indeed, for miniature art, gesso possesses innumerable advantages not presented by any other medium, but it is hardly available for larger works.

Time and space will not permit my entering more fully into these two forms of plastic art; but seeing that we are annually receiving such large accessions to the numbers of our modellers, and as, of course, it is not possible for all these to achieve success in, or find a means of living by, the art of sculpture in marble, I have sought to indicate a home-art means by which, at very moderate cost, they can bring their labours in useful form before the world, and at the same time learn and live.

G. T. Robinson.

OF CAST IRON

CAST iron is nearly our humblest material, and with associations less than all artistic, for it has been almost hopelessly vulgarised in the present century, so much so that Mr. Ruskin, with his fearless use of paradox to shock one into thought, has laid it down that cast iron is an artistic solecism, impossible for architectural service now, or at any time. And yet, although we can never claim for iron the beauty of bronze, it is in some degree a parallel material, and has been used with appreciation in many ways up to the beginning of this century.

Of Cast Iron.

Iron was already known in Sussex at the coming of the Romans. Throughout this county and Kent, in out-of-the-way farm-houses, iron fire-backs to open hearths, fine specimens of the founder's art, are still in daily use as they have been for three hundred years or more. Some have Gothic diapers and meanders of vine with heraldic badges and initials, and are evidently cast from models made in the fifteenth century, patterns that remained in stock and were cast from again and again. Others, of the following centuries, have coat-arms and supporters, salamanders in the flames, figures, a triton or centaur, or even a scene, the Judgment of Solomon, or Marriage of Alexander, or, more appropriately, mere pattern-work, vases of flowers and the like. However crude they may be, and some are absurdly inadequate as sculpture, the sense of treatment and relief suitable to the material never fails to give them a fit interest.

With these backs cast-iron fire-dogs are often found, of which some Gothic examples also remain, simple in form with soft dull modelling; later, these were often a mere obelisk on a base surmounted by a ball or a bird, or rude terminal figures; sometimes a more delicate full figure, the limbs well together, so that nothing projects from the general post-like form; and within their limitations they are not without grace and character.

In Frant church, near Tunbridge, are several cast-iron grave slabs about six feet long by half that width, perfectly flat, one with a single shield of arms and some letters, others with several; they are quite successful, natural, and not in the least vulgar.

Iron railings are the most usual form

of cast iron as an accessory to architecture; the earlier examples of these in London are thoroughly fit for their purpose and their material; sturdily simple forms of gently swelling curves, or with slightly rounded reliefs. The original railing at St. Paul's, of Lamberhurst iron, is the finest of these, a large portion of which around the west front was removed in 1873. Another example encloses the portico of St. Martin's-in-the-Fields. The railing of the central area of Berkeley Square is beautifully designed, and there are instances here, as in Grosvenor Square, where cast iron is used together with wrought, a difficult combination.

Of Cast Iron.

Balcony railings and staircase balustrades are quite general to houses of the late eighteenth century. Refined and thoroughly good of their kind, they never fail to please, and never, of course, imitate wrought iron. The design is always direct, unpretentious and effortless, in a manner that became at this time quite a tradition.

The verandahs also, of which there are so many in Piccadilly or Mayfair, with posts reeded and of delicate profiles, are of the same kind, confessedly cast iron, and never without the characterising dulness of the forms, so that they have no jutting members to be broken off, to expose a repulsive jagged fracture. The opposite of all these qualities may be found in the "expensive"-looking railing on the Embankment enclosing the gardens, whose tiny fretted and fretful forms invite an experiment often successful.

It must be understood that cast iron should be merely a flat lattice-like design, obviously cast *in panels*, or plain post and rail construction with cast uprights and terminal knops tenoned into rails, so that there is no doubt of straightforward unaffected fitting. The British Museum screen may be taken to instance how ample ability will not redeem false principles of design: the construction is not clear, nor are the forms sufficiently simple, the result being only a high order of commonplace grandeur.

Even the lamp-posts set up in the beginning of the century for oil lights, a few of which have not yet been improved away from back streets, show the same care for appropriate form. Some of the Pall Mall Clubs, again, have well-designed candelabra of a more pretentious kind; also London and Waterloo Bridges.

The fire-grates, both with hobs and close fronts, that came into use about the middle of the last century, are decorated all over the field with tiny flutings, beads, and leaf mouldings, sometimes

Of Cast Iron.

even with little figure medallions, and carry delicacy to its limit. The better examples are entirely successful, both in form and in the ornamentation, which, adapted to this new purpose, does no more than gracefully acknowledge its debt to the past, just as the best ornament at all times is neither original nor copied: it must recognise tradition, and add something which shall be the tradition of the future. The method followed is to keep the general form quite simple and the areas flat, while the decoration, just an embroidery of the surface, is of one substance and in the slightest possible relief. Other larger grates there were with plain surfaces simply framed with mouldings.

Even the sculptor has not refused iron. Pliny says there were two statues in Rhodes, one of iron and copper, and the other, a Hercules, entirely of iron. In the palace at Prague there is a St. George horsed and armed, the work of the fourteenth century. The qualities natural to iron which it has to offer for sculpture may best be appreciated by seeing the examples at the Museum of Geology, in Jermyn Street. On the staircase there are two large dogs, two ornamental candelabra, and two figures; the dogs, although not fine as sculpture, are well treated, in mass and surface, for the metal. In the same museum there is a smaller statue still better for surface and finish, a French work signed and dated 1841, and, therefore, half an antique. But for ordinary foundry-work without surface finish—probably the most appropriate, certainly the most available, method—the little lions on the outer rail at the British Museum are proof of how sufficient feeling for design will dignify any material for any object;

Of Cast Iron.

they are by the late Alfred Stevens, and are thoroughly iron beasts, so slightly modelled that they would be only blocked out for bronze. In the Geological Museum are also specimens of Berlin and Ilsenburg manufacture; they serve to point the moral that ingenuity is not art, nor tenuity refinement.

The question of rust is a difficult one, the oxide not being an added beauty like the patina acquired by bronze, yet the decay of cast iron is much less than is generally thought, especially on large smooth surfaces, if the casting has been once treated by an oil bath or a coating of hot tar: the celebrated iron pillar of Delhi, some twenty feet high, has stood for fourteen centuries, and shows, it is said, little evidence of decay. It would be interesting to see how cast spheres of good iron would be affected in our climate, if occasionally coated with a lacquer. In painting, the range of tints best approved is black through gray to white: the simple negative gray gives a pleasant unobtrusiveness to the well-designed iron-work of the Northern Station in Paris, whereas our almost universal Indian red is a very bad choice—a hot coarse colour, you must see it, and be irritated, and it is surely the only colour that gets worse as it bleaches in the sun. Gilding is suitable to a certain extent; but for internal work the homely black-leading cannot be bettered.

Of Cast Iron.

To put together the results obtained in our examination of examples.

(1) The metal must be both good and carefully manipulated.

(2) The design must be thought out through the material and its traditional methods.

(3) The pattern must have the ornament modelled, not carved, as is almost

universally the case now, carving in wood being entirely unfit to give the soft suggestive relief required both by the nature of the sand-mould into which it is impressed, and the crystalline structure of the metal when cast.

(4) Flat surfaces like grate fronts may be decorated with some intricacy if the relief is delicate. But the relief must be less than the basis of attachment, so that the moulding may be easily practicable, and no portions invite one to test how easily they might be detached.

(5) Objects in the round must have a simple and substantial bounding form with but little ornament, and that only suggested. This applies equally to figures. In them homogeneous structure is of the first importance.

(6) When possible, the surface should be finished and left as a metal casting. It may, however, be entirely gilt. If

painted, the colour must be neutral and gray.

Casting in iron has been so abased and abused that it is almost difficult to believe that the metal has anything to offer to the arts. At no other time and in no other country would a national staple commodity have been so degraded. Yet in its strength under pressure, but fragility to a blow, in certain qualities of texture and of required manipulation, it invites a specially characterised treatment in the design, and it offers one of the few materials naturally black available in the colour arrangement of interiors.

W. R. Lethaby.

OF DYEING AS AN ART

DYEING is a very ancient art; from the earliest times of the ancient civilisations till within about forty years ago there had been no essential change in it, and not much change of any kind. Up to the time of the discovery of the process of Prussian-blue dyeing in about 1810 (it was known as a pigment thirty or forty years earlier), the only changes in the art were the result of the introduction of the American insect dye (cochineal), which gradually superseded the European one (kermes), and the American wood-dyes now known as logwood and Brazil-wood: the latter differs little from the Asiatic and African Red Saunders, and other red dye-woods; the former has cheapened and worsened black-dyeing, in so far as it has taken the place of the indigo-vat as a basis. The American quercitron bark gives us also a useful additional yellow dye.

These changes, and one or two others, however, did little towards revolutionising the art; that revolution was left for our own days, and resulted from the discovery of what are known as the Aniline dyes, deduced by a long process from the plants of the coal-measures. Of these dyes it must be enough to say that their discovery, while conferring the greatest honour on the abstract science of chemistry, and while doing great service to capitalists in their hunt after profits, has terribly injured the art of dyeing, and for the general public has nearly destroyed

Of Dyeing as an Art.

it as an art. Henceforward there is an absolute divorce between the *commercial process* and the *art* of dyeing. Any one wanting to produce dyed textiles with any artistic quality in them must entirely forgo the modern and commercial methods in favour of those which are at least as old as Pliny, who speaks of them as being old in his time.

Now, in order to dye textiles in patterns or otherwise, we need four colours to start with—to wit, blue, red, yellow, and brown ; green, purple, black, and all intermediate shades can be made from a mixture of these colours.

Blue is given us by indigo and woad, which do not differ in colour in the least, their chemical product being the same. Woad may be called northern indigo ; and indigo tropical or sub-tropical woad.

Note that until the introduction of Prussian blue about 1810 there was *no* other blue dye except this indigotine that could be called a dye; the other blue dyes were mere stains which would not bear the sun for more than a few days.

Red is yielded by the insect dyes kermes, lac-dye, and cochineal, and by the vegetable dye madder. Of these, kermes is the king; brighter than madder and at once more permanent and more beautiful than cochineal: the latter on an aluminous basis gives a rather cold crimson, and on a tin basis a rather hot scarlet (*e.g.* the dress-coat of a line officer). Madder yields on wool a deep-toned blood-red, somewhat bricky and tending to scarlet. On cotton and linen, all imaginable shades of red according to the process. It is not of much use in dyeing silk, which it is apt to "blind"; *i.e.* it takes off the gloss. Lac-dye gives a hot and not pleasant scarlet, as may be noted in a private militiaman's coat. The French liners' trousers, by the way, are, or were, dyed with madder, so that their countrymen sometimes call them the "Madder-wearers"; but their cloth is somewhat too cheaply dyed to do credit to the drysaltery.

Besides these permanent red dyes there are others produced from woods, called in the Middle Ages by the general name of "Brazil"; whence the name of the American country, because the conquerors found so much dyeing-wood growing there. Some of these wood-dyes are very beautiful in colour; but unluckily they are none of them permanent, as you may see by examining the beautiful stuffs of the thirteenth and fourteenth centuries at the South Kensington Museum, in which you will scarcely find any red, but plenty of fawn-colour, which is in fact the wood-red of 500 years ago thus faded. If you turn from them to the Gothic tapestries, and note the reds in them, you will have the measure of the relative permanence of kermes and "Brazil," the tapestry reds being all dyed with kermes, and still retaining the greater part of their colour. The mediæval dyers must be partly excused, however, because "Brazil" is especially a silk dye, kermes sharing somewhat in the ill qualities of madder for silk; though I have dyed silk in kermes and got very beautiful and powerful colours by means of it.

Yellow dyes are chiefly given us by weld (sometimes called wild mignonette), quercitron bark (above mentioned), and old fustic, an American dye-wood. Of these weld is much the prettiest, and is the yellow silk dye *par excellence*, though it dyes wool well enough. But yellow dyes are the commonest to be met with in nature, and our fields and hedgerows bear plenty of greening-weeds, as our forefathers called them, since they used them chiefly for greening blue woollen cloth ; for, as you may well believe, they, being good colourists, had no great taste for yellow woollen stuff. Dyers'-broom, saw-wort, the twigs of the poplar, the osier, and the birch, heather, broom, flowers and twigs, will all of them give yellows of more or less permanence. Of these I have tried poplar and osier twigs, which both gave a strong yellow, but the former not a very permanent one.

Speaking generally, yellow dyes are the least permanent of all, as once more you may see by looking at an old tapestry, in which the greens have always faded more than the reds or blues ; the best yellow dyes, however, lose only their brighter shade, the "lemon" colour, and leave a residuum of brownish yellow, which still makes a kind of a green over the blue.

Brown is best got from the roots of the walnut tree, or in their default from the green husks of the nuts. This material is especially best for "saddening," as the old dyers used to call it. The best and most enduring blacks also were done with this simple dye-stuff, the goods being first dyed in the indigo or woad-vat till they were a very dark blue and then browned into black by means of the walnut-root. Catechu, the inspissated juice of a plant or plants, which comes to us from India, also gives rich and useful permanent browns of various shades.

Green is obtained by dyeing a blue of the required shade in the indigo-vat, and then greening it with a good yellow dye, adding what else may be necessary (as, *e.g.*, madder) to modify the colour according to taste.

Purple is got by blueing in the indigo-vat, and afterwards by a bath of cochineal, or kermes, or madder; all intermediate shades of claret and murrey and russet can be got by these drugs helped out by "saddening."

Black, as aforesaid, is best made by dyeing dark blue wool with brown; and walnut is better than iron for the brown part, because the iron-brown is apt to rot the fibre; as once more you will see in some pieces of old tapestry or old Persian carpets, where the black is quite perished, or at least in the case of the carpet gone down to the knots. All intermediate shades can, as aforesaid, be got by the blending of these prime colours, or by using weak baths of them. For instance, all shades of flesh colour can be got by means of weak baths of madder and walnut "saddening"; madder or cochineal mixed with weld gives us orange, and with saddening all imaginable shades between yellow and red, including the ambers, maize-colour, etc. The crimsons in Gothic tapestries must have been got by dyeing kermes over pale shades of blue, since the crimson red-dye, cochineal, had not yet come to Europe.

A word or two (entirely unscientific) about the processes of this old-fashioned or artistic dyeing.

In the first place, all *dyes* must be soluble colours, differing in this respect from *pigments*; most of which are insoluble, and are only very finely divided, as, *e.g.*, ultramarine, umber, terre-verte.

Next, dyes may be divided into those which need a mordant and those which do not; or, as the old chemist Bancroft very conveniently expresses it, into *adjective* and *substantive* dyes.

Indigo is the great substantive dye: the indigo has to be de-oxidised and thereby made soluble, in which state it loses its blue colour in proportion as the solution is complete; the goods are plunged into this solution and worked in it "between two waters," as the phrase goes, and when exposed to the air the indigo they have got on them is swiftly oxidised, and once more becomes insoluble. This process is repeated till the required shade is got. All shades of blue can be got by this means, from the pale "watchet," as our forefathers called it, up to the blue which the eighteenth-century French dyers called "Bleu d'enfer." Navy Blue is the politer name for it to-day in England. I must add that, though this seems an easy process, the setting of the blue-vat is a ticklish job, and requires, I should say, more experience than any other dyeing process.

The brown dyes, walnut and catechu, need no mordant, and are substantive dyes; some of the yellows also can be dyed without mordant, but are much improved by it. The red dyes, kermes and madder, and the yellow dye weld, are especially mordant or adjective dyes: they are all dyed on an aluminous basis. To put the matter plainly, the goods are worked in a solution of alum (usually with a little acid added), and after an interval of a day or two (ageing) are dyed in a bath of the dissolved dye-stuff.

A lake is thus formed on the fibre which is in most cases very durable. The effect of this "mordanting" of the fibre is clearest seen in the maddering of printed cotton goods, which are first printed with aluminous mordants of various degrees of strength (or with iron if black is needed, or a mixture of iron with alumina for purple), and then dyed wholesale in the madder-beck: the result being that the parts which have been mordanted come out various shades of red, etc., according to the strength or composition of the mordant, while the unmordanted parts remain a dirty pink, which has to be "cleared" into white by soaping and exposure to the sun and air; which process both brightens and fixes the dyed parts.

Pliny saw this going on in Egypt, and it puzzled him very much, that a cloth dyed in one colour should come out coloured diversely.

That reminds me to say a word on the fish-dye of the ancients: it was a substantive dye and behaved somewhat as indigo. It was very permanent. The colour was a real purple in the modern sense of the word, *i.e.* a colour or shades of a colour between red and blue. The real Byzantine books which are written on purple vellum give you some, at least, of its shades. The ancients, you must remember, used words for colours in a way that seems vague to us, because they were generally thinking of the tone rather than the *tint*. When they wanted to *specify* a red dye they would not use the word purpureus, but coccineus, *i.e.* scarlet of kermes.

Of Dyeing as an Art.

The art of dyeing, I am bound to say, is a difficult one, needing for its practice a good craftsman, with plenty of experience. Matching a colour by means of it is an agreeable but somewhat anxious game to play.

As to the artistic value of these dye-stuffs, most of which, together with the necessary mordant alumina, the world discovered in early times (I mean early *historical* times), I must tell you that they all make in their simplest forms beautiful colours; they need no muddling into artistic usefulness, when you need your colours bright (as I hope you usually do), and they can be modified and toned without dirtying, as the foul blotches of the capitalist dyer cannot be. Like all dyes, they are not eternal; the sun in lighting them and beautifying them consumes them; yet gradually, and for the most part kindly, as (to use my example for the last time in this paper) you will see if you look at the Gothic tapestries in the drawing-room at Hampton Court. These colours in fading still remain beautiful, and never, even after long wear, pass into nothingness, through that stage of livid ugliness which distinguishes the commercial dyes as nuisances, even more than their short and by no means merry life.

I may also note that no textiles dyed blue or green, otherwise than by indigo, keep an agreeable colour by candle-light: many quite bright greens turning into sheer drab. A fashionable blue which simulates indigo turns into a slaty purple by candle-light; and Prussian blues are also much damaged by it. I except from this condemnation a commercial green known as gas-green, which is as abominable as its name, both by daylight and gaslight, and indeed one would almost expect it to make unlighted midnight hideous.

William Morris.

OF EMBROIDERY

THE technicalities of Embroidery are very simple and its tools few—practically consisting of a needle, and nothing else. The work can be wrought loose in the hand, or stretched in a frame, which latter mode is often advisable, always when smooth and minute work is aimed at. There are no mysteries of method beyond a few elementary rules that can be quickly learnt; no way to perfection except that of care and patience and love of the work itself. This being so, the more is demanded from design and execution: we look for complete triumph over the limitations of process and material, and, what is equally important, a certain judgment and self-restraint; and, in short, those mental qualities that distinguish mechanical from intelligent work. The latitude allowed to the worker; the lavishness and ingenuity displayed in the stitches employed; in short, the vivid expression of the worker's individuality, form a great part of the success of needlework.

The varieties of stitch are too many to be closely described without diagrams, but the chief are as follows:—

Chain-stitch consists of loops simulating the links of a simple chain. Some of the most famous work of the Middle Ages was worked in this stitch, which is enduring, and of its nature necessitates careful execution. We are more familiar with it in the dainty work of the seventeenth and eighteenth centuries, in the airy brightness and simplicity of which lies a peculiar charm, contrasted with the more pompous and pretentious work of the same period. This stitch is also wrought with a hook on any loose material stretched in a tambour frame.

Tapestry-stitch consists of a building-up of stitches laid one beside another, and gives a surface slightly resembling that of tapestry. I give the name as it is so often used, but it is vague, and leads to the confusion that exists in people's minds between loom-tapestry and embroidery. The stitch is worked in a frame, and is particularly suitable for the drapery of figures and anything that requires skilful blending of several colours, or a certain amount of shading. This facility of "painting" with the needle is in itself a danger, for it tempts some people to produce a highly shaded imitation of a picture, an attempt which must be a failure both as a decorative and as a pictorial achievement. It cannot be said too often that the essential qualities of all good needlework are a broad surface, bold lines and pure, brilliant and, as a rule, simple colouring; all of which being qualities attainable through, and prescribed by, the limitations of this art.

Appliqué has been, and is still, a favourite method of work, which Vasari tells us Botticelli praised as being very suitable to processional banners and hangings used in the open air, as it is solid and enduring, also bold and effective in style. It is more accurately described as a *method* of work in which various stitches are made use of, for it consists of designs embroidered on a stout ground and then cut out and laid on silk or velvet, and edged round with lines of gold or silk, and sometimes with pearls. It requires considerable deftness and judgment in applying, as the work could well be spoilt by clumsy and heavy finishing. It is now looked upon as solely ecclesiastical, I believe, and is associated in our minds with garish red, gold and white, and with dull geometric ornament, though there is absolutely no reason why church embroidery of to-day should be limited to ungraceful forms and staring colours. A certain period of work, thick and solid, but not very interesting, either as to method or design, has been stereotyped into what is known as Ecclesiastical Embroidery, the mechanical characteristics of the style being, of course, emphasised and exaggerated in the process. Church work will never be of the finest while these characteristics are insisted on; the more pity, as it is seemly that the richest and noblest work should be devoted to churches, and to all buildings that belong to and are an expression of the communal life of the people. Another and simpler form of applied work is to cut out the desired forms in one material and lay upon another, securing the appliqué with stitches round the outline, which are hidden by an edging cord. The work may be further enriched by light ornament of lines and flourishes laid directly on the ground material.

Couching is an effective method of work, in which broad masses of silk or gold thread are laid down and secured by a network or diaper of crossing threads, through which the under surface shines very prettily. It is often used in conjunction with appliqué. There are as many varieties of couching stitches as the worker has invention for ; in some the threads are laid simply and flatly on the form to be covered, while in others a slight relief is obtained by layers of soft linen thread which form a kind of moulding or stuffing, and which are covered by the silk threads or whatever is to be the final decorative surface.

The ingenious patchwork coverlets of our grandmothers, formed of scraps of old gowns pieced together in certain symmetrical forms, constitute the romance of family history, but this method has an older origin than would be imagined. Queen Isis-em-Kheb's embalmed body went down the Nile to its burial-place under a canopy that was lately discovered, and is preserved in the Boulak Museum. It consists of many squares of gazelle-hide of different colours sewn together and ornamented with various devices. Under the name of patchwork, or mosaic-like piecing together of different coloured stuffs, comes also the Persian work made at Resht. Bits of fine cloth are cut out for leaves, flowers, and so forth, and neatly stitched together with great accuracy. This done, the work is further carried out and enriched by chain and other stitches. The result is perfectly smooth flat work, no easy feat when done on a large scale, as it often is.

Darning and running need little explanation. The former stitch is familiar to us in the well-known Cretan and Turkish cloths: the stitch here is used mechanically in parallel lines, and simulates weaving, so that these handsome borders in a deep rich red might as well have come from the loom as from the needle. Another method of darning is looser and coarser, and suitable only for cloths and hangings not subject to much wear and rubbing; the stitches follow the curves of the design, which the needle paints, as it were, shading and blending the colours. It is necessary to use this facility for shading temperately, however, or the flatness essential to decorative work is lost.

The foregoing is a rough list of stitches which could be copiously supplemented, but that I am obliged to pass on to another important point, that of design. If needlework is to be looked upon seriously, it is necessary to secure appropriate and practicable designs. Where the worker does not invent for herself, she should at least interpret her designer, just as the designer interprets and does not attempt to imitate nature. It follows from this, that it is better to avoid using designs of artists who know nothing of the capacities of needlework, and design beautiful and intricate forms without reference to the execution, the result being unsatisfactory and incomplete. Regarding the design itself, broad bold lines should be chosen, and broad harmonious colour (which should be roughly planned before setting to work), with as much minute work, and stitches introducing play of colour, as befits the purpose of the work and humour of the worker; there should be no scratching, no indefiniteness of form or colour, no vagueness that allows the eye to puzzle over the design—beyond that indefinable sense of mystery which arrests the attention and withholds the full charm of the work for a moment, to unfold it to those who stop to give it more than a glance. But there are so many different stitches and so many different modes of setting to work, that it will soon be seen that these few hints do not apply to all of them. One method, for instance, consists of trusting entirely to design, and leaves colour out of account: white work on white linen, white on dark ground, or black or dark blue upon white. Again, some work depends more on magnificence of colour than on form, as, for example, the handsome Italian hangings of the seventeenth century, worked in floss-silk, on linen sometimes, and sometimes on a dusky open canvas which makes the silks gleam and glow like precious stones.

In thus slightly describing the methods chiefly used in embroidery, I do so principally from old examples, as modern embroidery, being a dilettante pastime, has little distinct character, and is, in its best points, usually imitative. Eastern work still retains the old professional skill, but beauty of colour is rapidly disappearing, and little attention is paid to durability of the dyes used. In speaking rather slightingly of modern needlework, I must add that its non-success is often due more to the use of poor materials than to want of skill in working. It is surely folly to waste time over work that looks shabby in a month. The worker should use judgment and thought to procure materials, not necessarily rich, but each good and genuine of its kind. Lastly, she should not be sparing of her own handiwork, for, while a slightly executed piece of work depends wholly on design, in one where the actual stitchery is more elaborate, but the design less masterly, the patience and thought lavished on it render it in a different way equally pleasing, and bring it more within the scope of the amateur.

MAY MORRIS.

OF LACE

LACE is a term freely used at the present time to describe various sorts of open ornament in thread work, the successful effect of which depends very much upon the contrasting of more or less closely-textured forms with grounds or intervening spaces filled in with meshes of equal size or with cross-ties, bars, etc. Whence it has come to pass that fabrics having an appearance of this description, such as embroideries upon nets, cut linen works, drawn thread works, and machine-woven counterfeits of lace-like fabrics, are frequently called laces. But they differ in make from those productions of certain specialised handicrafts to which from the sixteenth to the eighteenth centuries lace owes its fame.

These specialised handicrafts are divisible into two branches. The one branch involves the employment of a needle to loop a continuous thread into varieties of shapes and devices; the other is in the nature of making corresponding or similar ornament by twisting and plaiting together a number of separate threads, the loose ends of which have to be fastened in a row on a cushion or pillow, the supply of the threads being wound around the heads of lengthened bobbins, so shaped for convenience in handling. The first-named branch is needlepoint lace-making; the second, bobbin or pillow lace-making. Needlepoint lace-making may be regarded as a species of embroidery, whilst bobbin or pillow lace-making is closely allied to the twisting and knotting together of threads for fringes. Embroidery, however, postulates a foundation of material to be enriched with needlework, whereas needlepoint and pillow lace are wrought independently of any corresponding foundation of material.

The production of slender needles and small metal pins is an important incident in the history of lace-making by hand. Broadly speaking, the manufacture for a widespread consumption of such metal pins and needles does not date earlier than the fourteenth century. Without small implements of this character delicate lace-making is not possible. It is therefore fair to assume that although historic nations like the Egyptian, Assyrian, Hebrew, Greek, and Roman, made use of fringes and knotted cords upon their hangings, cloaks, and tunics, lace was unknown to them. Their bone, wooden, or metal pins and needles were suited to certain classes of embroidery and to the making of nets, looped cords, etc., but not to such lace-making as we know it from the early days of the sixteenth century.

About the end of the fifteenth century, with the development in Europe of fine linen for underclothing, collars and cuffs just visible beyond the outer garments came into vogue, and a taste was speedily manifested for trimming linen undershirts, collars and cuffs, with insertions and borders of kindred material. This taste seems to have been first displayed in a marked manner by Venetian and Flemish women; for the earliest known books of engraved patterns for linen ornamental borders and insertions are those which were published during the commencement of the sixteenth century at Venice and Antwerp. But such patterns were designed in the first place for various sorts of embroidery upon a material, such as darning upon canvas (*punto fa su la rete a maglia quadra*), drawn thread work of reticulated patterns (*punto tirato* or *punto a reticella*), and cut work (*punto tagliato*). Patterns for quite other sorts of work, such as point in the air (*punto in aere*) and thread work twisted and plaited by means of little leaden weights or bobbins (*merletti a piombini*), were about thirty years later in publication. These two last-named classes of work are respectively identifiable (*punto in aere*) with needlepoint and (*merletti a piombini*) with bobbin lace-making; and they seem to date from about 1540.

The sixteenth-century and earliest known needlepoint laces (*punto in aere*) are of narrow lengths or bands, the patterns of which are composed principally of repeated open squares filled in with circular, star, and other geometric shapes, set upon diagonal and cross lines which radiate from the centre of each square to its corners and sides. When the bands were to serve as borders they would have a dentated edging added to them; this edging might be made of either needlepoint or bobbin lace. As time went on the dimensions of both lace bands and lace vandykes increased so that, whilst these served as trimmings to linen, lace of considerable width and various shapes came to be made, and ruffs, collars, and cuffs were wholly made of it. Such lace was thin and wiry in appearance. The leading lines of the patterns formed squares and geometrical figures, amongst which were disposed small wheel and seed forms, little triangles, and such like.

A few years later the details of these geometrically planned patterns became more varied, tiny human figures, fruits, vases and flowers, being used as ornamental details. But a more distinct change in character of pattern was effected when flowing scrolls with leaf and blossom devices, held together by means of little ties or bars, were adopted. Different portions of the scrolls and blossoms with their connecting links or bars would often be enriched with little loops or *picots*, with stitched reliefs, and varieties of close and open work. Then came a taste for arranging the bars or ties into trellis grounds, or grounds of hexagons, over which small ornamental devices would be scattered in balanced groups. At the same time, the bobbin or pillow lace-workers produced grounds of small equal-size meshes in plaited threads. This inventiveness on the part of the bobbin or pillow workers reacted upon the needlepoint workers, who in their turn produced still more delicate grounds with meshes of single and double twisted threads.

Lace, passing from stage to stage, thus became a filmy tissue or fabric, and its original use as a somewhat stiff, wiry-looking trimming to linen consequently changed. Larger articles than borders, collars, and cuffs were made of the new filmy material, and lace flounces, veils, loose sleeves, curtains, and bed-covers were produced. This transition may be traced through the first hundred and twenty years of lace-making. It culminated during the succeeding ninety years in a development of fanciful pattern-making, in which realistic representation of flowers, trees, cupids, warriors, sportsmen, animals of the chase, emblems of all sorts, rococo and architectural ornament, is typical. Whilst the eighteenth century may perhaps be regarded as a period of questionable propriety in the employment of ornament hardly appropriate to the twisting, plaiting, and looping together of threads, it is nevertheless notable for *tours de force* in lace-making achieved without regard to cost or trouble. From this stage, the climax of which may be placed about 1760, the designing of lace patterns declined; and from the end of the eighteenth to the first twenty years or so of the nineteenth centuries, laces, although still made with the needle and bobbins, became little more than finely-meshed nets powdered over with dots or leaves, or single blossoms, or tiny sprays.

Within the limits of a brief note like the present, it is not possible to discuss local peculiarities in methods of work and styles of design which established the characters of the various Venetian and other Italian points, of the French points of Alençon and Argentan, of the cloudy Valenciennes, Mechlin, and Brussels laces. Neither can one touch upon the nurturing of the industry by nuns in convents, by workers subsidised by State grants, and so forth. It would require more space than is available to fairly discuss what styles of ornament are least or most suited to lace-making ; or whether lace is less rightly employed as a tissue for the making of entire articles of costume or of household use, than as an ornamental accessory or trimming to costume.

Whilst very much lace is a fantastic adjunct to costume, serving a purpose sometimes like that of *appoggiature* and *fioriture* in music, other lace, such as the carved-ivory-looking scrolls of Venetian raised points, which are principally associated with the *jabots* and ruffles of kings, ministers, and marshals, and with the ornamentation of priests' vestments, is certainly more dignified in character. The loops, twists, and plaits of threads are more noticeable in laces of comparatively small dimensions than they are in laces of great size. Size rather tempts the lace-worker to strive for ready effect, and to sacrifice the minuteness and finish of hand work, which give quality of preciousness to lace. The *via media* to this quality lies between two extremes; namely, applying dainty threads to the interpretation of badly shaped and ill-grouped forms on the one hand, and on the other hand adopting a style of ornament which depends upon largeness of detail and massiveness in grouping, and is therefore unsuited to lace. Without finish of handicraft, producing beautiful ornament suited to the material in which it is expressed, lace worthy the name cannot be made.

The industry is still pursued in France, Belgium, Venice, Austria, Bohemia, and Ireland. Honiton has acquired a notoriety for its pillow laces, many of which some hundred years ago were as varied and well executed as Brussels pillow laces. Other English towns in the Midland counties followed the lead chiefly of Mechlin, Valenciennes, Lille, and Arras, but were rarely as successful as their leaders. Saxony, Russia, and the Auvergne produce quantities of pillow laces, having little pretence to design, though capable of pretty effects when artistically worn. There is no question that the want of a sustained intelligence in appreciating ingenious hand-made laces has told severely upon the industry; and as with other artistic handicrafts, so with

Of Lace. lace-making, machinery has very considerably supplanted the hand. There is at present a limited revival in the demand for hand-made laces, and efforts are made at certain centres to give new life to the industry by infusing into it artistic feeling derived from a study of work done during the periods when the art flourished.

ALAN S. COLE.

OF BOOK ILLUSTRATION AND BOOK DECORATION

BOOK illustration is supposed to have made a great advance in the last few years. No doubt it has, but this advance has not been made on any definite principle, but, as it were, in and out of a network of cross-purposes. No attempt has been made to classify illustration in relation to the purpose it has to fulfil.

Broadly speaking, this purpose is threefold. It is either utilitarian, or partly utilitarian partly artistic, or purely artistic. The first may be dismissed at once. Such drawings as technical diagrams must be clear and accurate, but by their very nature they are non-artistic, and in regard to art it is a case of "hands off" to the draughtsman.

Illustration as an art, that is, book decoration, begins with the second class. From this standpoint an illustration involves something more than mere drawing. In the first place, the drawing must illustrate the subject, but as the drawing will not be set in a plain mount, but surrounded or bordered by printed type, there is the further problem of the relation of the drawing to the printed type. The relative importance attached to the printed type or the drawing is the crucial point for the illustrator. If all his thoughts are concentrated on his own drawing, one line to him will be much as another; but if he considers his illustration as going with the type to form one homogeneous design, each line becomes a matter of deliberate intention.

Now, in the early days of printing, when both type and illustration were printed off a single block, the latter standpoint was adopted as a matter of course, and as the art developed and men of genuine ability applied themselves to design, this intimate relation between printer and designer produced results of inimitable beauty. Each page of a fine Aldine is a work of art in itself. The eye can run over page after page for the simple pleasure of its decoration. No black blots in a sea of ignoble type break the quiet dignity of the page; each part of it works together with the rest for one premeditated harmony. But gradually, with the severance of the arts, the printer lost sight of the artist, and the latter cared only for himself; and there came the inevitable result which has followed this selfishness in all the other arts of design. Printing ceased to be an art at all, and the art of book decoration died of neglect; the illustrator made his drawing without thought of the type, and left it to the printer to pitch it into the text, and reproduce it as best he could.

The low-water mark in artistic illustration was reached perhaps in the early part of this century, and the greatest offender was Turner himself. The illustrations which Turner made for Rogers's Poems show no sort of modification of his habitual practice in painting. They may have been beautiful in themselves, but it evidently never entered into Turner's head that the method, which was admirable in a picture aided by all the resources of colour, was beside the mark when applied to the printed page with all the limitations of black and white and the simple line. One looks in vain in Turner's illustrations for any evidence that he was conscious of the existence of the rest of the page at all. Something more than a landscape painter's knowledge of drawing is necessary. The custom of getting illustrations from painters who have little knowledge of decorative design has led to the invention of all sorts of mechanical processes in order to transfer easel-work direct to the printed page. The effect of this upon book decoration has been deadly. Process-work of this sort has gone far to kill wood-engraving; and as to its result, instead of a uniform texture of line woven as it were over the entire page, the eye is arrested by harsh patches of black or gray which show a disregard of the printed type which is little less than brutal. Leaving recent work out of account, one exception only can be made, and that is in the case of William Blake.

The inherent conditions of book decoration point to the line drawn by hand, and reproduced, either by wood-engraving or by direct facsimile process, as its proper method. Indeed, the ideal of paginal beauty would be reached by leaving both the text and the illustrative design to hand, if not to one hand. This, however, is out of the question; the cost alone is prohibitive. The point for the book-decorator to consider is, what sort of line will range best with the type. In the case of the second division of our classification, which, in default of a better name, may be called "record work," it is impossible to apply to the line the amount of abstraction and selection which would be necessary in pure design. To do so, for instance, in the case of an architectural illustration, would destroy the "vraisemblance" which is of the essence of such a drawing. Even in this case, however, the line ought to be very carefully considered. It is important to recollect that the type establishes a sort of scale of its own, and, taking ordinary lettering, this would exclude very minute work where the lines are close together and there is much cross-hatching; and also simple outline work such as Retsch used to labour at, for the latter errs on the side of tenuity and meagreness as much as process-reproduction of brush-work sins in the opposite extreme. The line used in architectural illustration should be free, accurate, and unfaltering, drawn with sufficient technical knowledge of architecture to enable the draughtsman to know where he can stop without injury to his subject. The line should not be obstinate, but so light and subtle as to reflect without effort each thought that flits across the artist's mind. Vierge has shown how much can be done in this way. With a few free lines and the contrast of some dark piece of shading in exactly the right place, he will often tell you more of a subject than will the most elaborately finished picture. This is the method to aim at in architectural illustration. The poetry of architecture and its highest qualities of dignity of mass and outline are smothered by that laborious accuracy which covers every part of the drawing with a vain repetition of unfeeling lines.

Where, however, the illustration is purely imaginative, the decorative standpoint should be kept steadily in view, and the process of selection and abstraction carried very much farther. Here, at length, the illustrator can so order his design that the drawing and the printed type form a single piece of decoration, not disregarding the type, but using it as in itself a means of obtaining texture and scale and distributed effect. The type is, as it were, the technical datum of the design, which determines the scale of the line to be used with it. With a wiry type no doubt a wiry drawing is desirable, but the types of the great periods of printing are firm in outline and large and ample in distribution. Assuming, then, that one of these types can be used, the line of the accompanying design should be strongly drawn, and designed from end to end with full allowance for the white paper. No better model can be followed than Dürer's woodcuts. The amount of work which Dürer would get out of a single line is something extraordinary, and perhaps to us impossible; for in view of our complex modern ideas and total absence of tradition, probably no modern designer can hope to attain to the great German's magnificent directness and tremendous intensity of expression.

Deliberate selection, both in subject and treatment, becomes therefore a matter of the first importance. The designer should reject subjects which do not admit of a decorative treatment. His business is not with science, or morals, but with art for its own sake; he should, therefore, select his subject with a single eye to its artistic possibilities. As to the line itself, it is impossible to offer any suggestion, for the line used is as much a part of the designer's idea as the words of a poem are of a poet's poetry; and the invention of these must come of itself. But once in consciousness, the line must be put under rigid control as simply a means of expression. There is an insidious danger in the line. Designers sometimes seem to be inebriated with their own cunning; they go on drawing line after line, apparently for the simple pleasure of deftly placing them side by side, or at best to produce some spurious imitation of texture. As soon as the line is made an end in itself, it becomes a wearisome thing. The use of the line and the imitation of texture should be absolutely subordinated to the decorative purposes of the design, and the neglect of this rule is as bad art as if a musician, from perverse delight in the intricacies of a fugue, were to lose his theme in a chaos of counterpoint.

If, then, to conclude, we are to return to the best traditions of book decoration, the artist must abandon the selfish isolation in which he has hitherto worked. He must regard the printed type not as a necessary evil, but as a valuable material for the decoration of the page, and the type and the illustration should be considered in strict relation to each other. This will involve a self-restraint far more rigid than any required in etching, because the point to be aimed at is not so much the direct suggestion of nature, as the best decorative treatment of the line in relation to the entire page. Thus, to the skill of the draughtsman must be added the far-seeing imagination of the designer, which, instead of being content with a hole-and-corner success, involving disgrace to the rest of the page, embraces in its consciousness all the materials available for the beautification of the page as a whole. It is only by this severe intellectual effort, by this self-abnegation, by this ready acceptance of the union of the arts, that the art of book illustration can again attain to a permanent value.

REGINALD BLOMFIELD.

OF DESIGNS AND WORKING DRAWINGS

THE drawings which most deeply interest the workman are working drawings—just the last to be appreciated by the public, because they are the last to be understood. The most admired of show drawings are to us craftsmen comparatively without interest. We recognise the "competition" drawing at once; we see how it was made in order to secure the commission, not with a view to its effect in execution (which is the true and only end of a design), and we do not wonder at the failure of competitions in general. For the man who cares least, if even he knows at all, how a design will appear in execution is the most likely to perpetrate a prettiness which may gain the favour of the inexpert, with whom the selection is likely to rest.

The general public, and all in fact who are technically ignorant on the subject, need to be warned that the most attractive and what are called "taking" drawings are just those which are least likely to be designs—still less *bonâ fide* working drawings. The real workman has not the time, even if he had the inclination, to "finish up" his drawings to the point that is generally considered pleasing; the inventive spirit has not the patience. We have each of us the failings complementary to our faculties, and *vice versâ;* and you will usually find—certainly it is my experience—that the makers of very elaborately finished drawings seldom do anything but what we have often seen before; and that men of any individuality, actual designers that is to say, have a way of considering a drawing finished as soon as ever it expresses what they mean.

You may take it, then, as a general rule that highly finished and elaborate drawings are got up for show, "finished for exhibition" as they say (in compliance with the supposed requirements of an exhibition rather than with a view to practical purposes), and that drawings completed only so far as is necessary, precise in their details, disfigured by notes in writing, sections, and so on, are at least genuine workaday designs.

If you ask what a design should be like—well, like a design. It is altogether a different thing from a picture; it is almost the reverse of it. Practically no man has, as I said, the leisure, even if he had the ability, to make an effective finished picture of a thing yet to be carried out—perhaps *not* to be carried out. This last is a most serious consideration for him, and may have a sad effect upon his work. The artist who could afford thus to give himself away gratis would certainly not do so; the man who might be willing to do it could not; for if he has "got no work to do"—that is at least presumptive evidence that he is not precisely a master of his craft.

The design that looks like a picture is likely to be at best a reminiscence of something done before; and the more often it has been done the more likely it is to be pictorially successful—and by so much the less is it, strictly speaking, a design.

This applies especially to designs on a

small scale, such as are usually submitted to catch the rare commission. To imitate in a full-sized cartoon the texture of material, the casualty of reflected light, and other such accidents of effect, is sheer nonsense, and no practical workman would think of such a thing. A painter put to the uncongenial task of decorative design might be excused for attempting to make his productions pass muster by workmanship excellent in itself, although not in the least to the point: one does what one can, or what one must; and if a man has a faculty he needs must show it. Only, the perfection of painting will not, for all that, make design.

Of Designs and Working Drawings.

In the first small sketch-design, everything need not of course be expressed; but it should be indicated—for the purpose is simply to explain the scheme proposed: so much of pictorial representation as may be necessary to that is desirable, and no more. It should be in the nature of a diagram, specific enough to illustrate the idea and how it is to be worked out. It ought by strict rights to commit one definitely to a certain method of execution, as a written specification would; and may often with advantage be helped out by written notes, which explain more definitely than any pictorial rendering just how this is to be wrought, that cast, the other chased, and so on, as the case may be.

Whatever the method of expression the artist may adopt, he should be perfectly clear in his own mind how his design is to be worked out; and he ought to make it clear also to any one with sufficient technical knowledge to understand a drawing.

In the first sketch for a window, for example, he need not show every lead and every piece of glass; but there should be no possible mistake as to how it is to be glazed, or which is "painted" glass and which is "mosaic." To omit the necessary bars in a sketch for glass seems to me a weak concession to the prejudice of the public. One *may* have to concede such points sometimes; but the concession is due less to necessity than to the—what shall we call it?—not perhaps exactly the cowardice, but at all events the timidity, of the artist.

In a full-sized working drawing or cartoon everything material to the design should be expressed, and that as definitely as possible. In a cartoon for glass (to take again the same example) every lead-line should be shown, as well as the saddle bars; to omit them is about as excusable as it would be to leave out the sections from a design for cabinet work. It is contended sometimes that such details are not necessary, that the artist can bear all that in mind. Doubtless he can, more or less; but I am inclined to believe more strongly in the *less*. At any rate he will much more certainly have them in view whilst he keeps them visibly before his eyes. One thing that deters him is the fear of offending the client, who will not believe, when he sees leads and bars in a drawing, how little they are likely to assert themselves in the glass.

Very much the same thing applies to designs and working drawings generally. A thorough craftsman never suggests a form or colour without realising in his own mind how he will be able to get such form or colour in the actual work; and in his working drawing he explains that fully, making allowance even for some not impossible dulness of apprehension on the part of the executant. Thus, if a pattern is to be woven he indicates the cards to be employed, he arranges what parts are "single," what "double," as the weavers call it, what changes in the shuttle are proposed, and by the crossing of which threads certain intermediate tints are to be obtained.

Or again, if the design is for wall-paper printing, he arranges not only for the blocks, but the order in which they shall be printed; and provides for possible printing in "flock," or for the printing of one transparent colour over another, so as to get more colours than there are blocks used, and so on.

In either case, too, he shows quite plainly the limits of each colour, not so much seeking the softness of effect which is his ultimate aim, as the precision which will enable the block or card cutter to see at a glance what he means,—even at the risk of a certain hardness in his drawing; for the drawing is in itself of no account; it is only the means to an end ; and his end is the stuff, the paper, or whatever it may be, in execution.

A workman intent on his design will sacrifice his drawing to it—harden it, as I said, for the sake of emphasis, annotate it, patch it, cut it up into pieces to prove it, if need be do anything to make his meaning clear to the workman who comes after him. It is as a rule only the dilettante who is dainty about preserving his drawings.

To an artist very much in repute there may be some temptation to be careful of his designs, and to elaborate them (himself, or by the hands of his assistants), because, so finished, they have a commercial value as drawings—but this is at best pot-boiling ; and the only men who are subject to this temptation are just those who might be proof against it. Men of such rank that even their working drawings are in demand have no very urgent need to work for the pot; and the working drawings of men to whom pounds and shillings must needs be a real consideration are not sought after.

Of Designs and Working Drawings.

In the case of very smart and highly finished drawings by comparatively unknown designers—of ninety-nine out of a hundred, that is to say, or nine hundred and ninety-nine out of a thousand perhaps—elaboration implies either that, having little to say, a man fills up his time in saying it at unnecessary length, or that he is working for exhibition.

And why not work for exhibition? it may be asked. There is a simple answer to that: The exhibition pitch is in much too high a key, and in the long run it will ruin the faculty of the workman who adopts it.

It is only fair to admit that an exhibition of fragmentary and unfinished drawings, soiled, tattered, and torn, as they almost invariably come from the workshop or factory, would make a very poor show—which may be an argument against exhibiting them at all. Certainly it is a reason for mending, cleaning, and mounting them, and putting them in some sort of frame (for what is not worth the pains of making presentable is not worth showing), but that is a very different thing from working designs up to picture pitch.

When all is said, designs, if exhibited, appeal primarily to designers. *We* all want to see each other's work, and especially each other's way of working ; but it should not be altogether uninteresting to the intelligent amateur to see what working drawings are, and to compare them with the kind of specious competition drawings by which he is so apt to be misled.

LEWIS F. DAY.

FURNITURE AND THE ROOM

THE art of furnishing runs on two wheels—the room and the furniture. As in the bicycle, the inordinate development of one wheel at the expense of its colleague has been not without some great feats, yet too often has provoked catastrophe; so furnishing makes safest progression when, with a juster proportion, its two wheels are kept to moderate and uniform diameters. The room should be for the furniture just as much as the furniture for the room.

Of late it has not been so; we have been indulging in the "disproportionately wheeled" type, and the result has been to crowd our rooms, and reduce them to insignificance. Even locomotion in them is often embarrassing, especially when the upholsterer has been allowed *carte blanche.* But, apart from this, there is a sense of repletion in these masses of chattel—miscellanies brought together with no subordination to each other, or to the effect of the room as a whole. Taken in the single piece, our furniture is sometimes not without its merit, but it is rarely exempt from self-assertion, or, to use a slang term, "fussiness." And an aggregation of "fussinesses" becomes fatiguing. One is betrayed into uncivilised longings for the workhouse, or even the convict's cell, the simplicity of bare boards and tables!

But we must not use our dictum for aggressive purposes merely, faulty as modern systems may be. In the distinction of the two sides of the problem of furnishing—the room for the furniture, and the furniture for the room—there is some historical significance. Under these titles might be written respectively the first and last chapters in the history of this art—its rise and its decadence.

Furniture and the Room.

Furniture in the embryonic state of chests, which held the possessions of early times, and served, as they moved from place to place, for tables, chairs, and wardrobes, may have been in existence while the tents and sheds which accommodated them were of less value. But furnishing began with settled architecture, when the room grew first into importance, and overshadowed its contents. The art of the builder had soared far beyond the ambitions of the furnisher.

Later, the two constituents of our art came to be produced simultaneously, and under one impulse of design. The room, whether church or hall, had now its specific furniture. In the former this was adapted for ritual, in the latter for feasting; but in both the contents formed in idea an integral part of the interior in which they stood. And while these conditions endured, the art was in its palmy state.

Later, furniture came to be considered apart from its position. It grew fanciful and fortuitous. The problem of fitting it to the room was no problem at all while both sprang from a common conception: it became so when its independent design, at first a foible of luxury, grew to be a necessity of production. As long, however, as architecture remained dominant, and painting and sculpture were its acknowledged vassals, furniture retained its legitimate position and shared in their triumphs. But when these the elder sisters shook off their allegiance, furniture followed suit. It developed the self-assertion of which we have spoken, and, in the belief that it could stand alone, divorced itself from that support which was the final cause of its existence. There have been doubtless many slackenings and tightenings of the chain which links the arts of design together; but it is to be noted how with each slackening furniture grew gorgeous and artificial, failed to sympathise with common needs, and sank slowly but surely into feebleness and insipidity.

We had passed through some such cycle by the middle of this century. With the dissolution of old ties the majority of the decorative arts had perished. Painting remained to us, arrogating to herself the rôle which hitherto the whole company had combined to make successful. In her struggle to fill the giant's robe, she has run unresistingly in the ruts of the age. She has crowded her portable canvases, side by side, into exhibitions and galleries, and claimed the title of art for literary rather than æsthetic suggestions. The minor coquetries of craftsmanship, from which once was nourished the burly strength of art, have felt out of place in such illustrious company. So we have the forced art of public display, but it has ceased to be the habit in which our common rooms and homely walls could be dressed.

The attendant symptom has been the loss from our houses of all that architectural amalgam, which in former times blended the structure with its contents, the screens and panellings, which, half room, half furniture, cemented the one to the other. The eighteenth century carried on the tradition to a great extent with plinth and dado, cornice and encrusted ceiling; but by the middle of the nineteenth we had our interiors handed over to us by the architect almost completely void of architectural feature. We are asked to take as a substitute, what is naïvely called "decoration," two coats of paint, and a veneer of machine-printed wall-papers.

In this progress of obliteration an important factor has been the increasing brevity of our tenures. Three or four times in twenty years the outgoing tenant will make good his dilapidations, and the house-agent will put the premises into tenantable repair—as these things are settled for us by lawyers and surveyors. After a series of such processes, what can remain of internal architecture?

Can there be left even a room worth furnishing, in the true sense of the term? The first step to render it so must usually be the obliteration of as much as possible of the maimed and distorted construction, which our leasehold house offers.

What wonder, then, if furniture, beginning again to account herself an art, should have transgressed her limits and invaded the room? Ceilings, walls and floors, chimneypieces, grates, doors and windows, all nowadays come into the hands of the artistic furnisher, and are at the mercy of upholsterers and cabinetmakers to begin with, and of the antiquity-collector to follow. Then we bring in our gardens, and finish off our drawing-room as a mixture of a conservatory and a bric-à-brac shop.

The fashion for archæological mimicry has been another pitfall. The attempt to bring back art by complete reproductions of old-day furnishings has been much the vogue abroad. The Parisians distinguish many styles and affect to carry them out in every detail. The Americans have copied Paris, and we have done a little ourselves. But the weak element in all this is, that the occupier of these mediæval or classic apartments remains still the nineteenth-century embodiment, which we meet in railway carriage and omnibus. We cannot be cultured Epicureans in a drawing-room of the Roman Empire, and by the opening of a door walk as Flemish Burgomasters into our libraries. The heart of the age will mould its productions irrespective of fashion or archæology, and such miserable shams fail to reach it.

If we, who live in this century, can at all ourselves appraise the position, its most essential characteristic in its bearing upon art has been the commercial tendency. Thereby an indelible stamp is set upon our furniture. The making of it under the supreme condition of profitable sale has affected it in both its functions. On the side of utility our furniture has been shaped to the uses of the million, not of the individual. Hence its monotonously average character, its failure to become part of ourselves, its lack of personal and local charm. How should a "stock" article possess either?

But the blight has fallen more cruelly on that other function, which is a necessity of human craftsmanship—the effort to express itself and please the eye by the expression. Art being the monopoly of "painting," and having nothing to do with such vulgar matters as furniture, commercialism has been able to advance a standard of beauty of its own, with one canon, that of speedy profits. Furniture has become a mere ware in the market of fashion. Bought to-day as the rage, it is discarded to-morrow, and some new fancy purchased. The tradesman has a new margin of profit, but the customer is just where he was. It may be granted that a genuine necessity of sale is the stimulus to which all serious effort in the arts must look for progress, and without which they would become faddism and conceit. But it is a different thing altogether when this passes from stimulus into motive — the exclusive motive of profit to the producer. The worth of the article is impaired as much as the well-being of the craftsman, and furniture is degraded to the position of a pawn in the game of the sweater.

We must, I fear, be content at

present to put up with exhibitions and unarchitectural rooms. But while making the best of these conditions, we need not acquiesce in them or maintain their permanence. At any rate we may fight a good fight with commercialism. The evils of heartless and unloving production, under the grind of an unnecessary greed, are patent enough to lead us to reflect that we have after all in these matters a choice. We need not spend our money on that which is not bread. We can go for our furniture to the individual craftsman and not the commercial firm. The penalty for so doing is no longer prohibitive.

In closing our remarks we cannot do better than repeat our initial axiom—the art of furnishing lies with the room as much as with the furniture. The old ways are still the only ways. When we care for art sufficiently to summon her from her state prison-house of exhibitions and galleries, to live again a free life among us in our homes, she will appear as a controlling force, using not only painting and sculpture, but all the decorative arts to shape room and furniture under one purpose of design. Whether we shall then give her the time-honoured title of architecture, or call her by another name, is of no moment.

EDWARD S. PRIOR.

OF THE ROOM AND FURNITURE

THE transient tenure that most of us have in our dwellings, and the absorbing nature of the struggle that most of us have to make to win the necessary provisions of life, prevent our encouraging the manufacture of well-wrought furniture.

We mean to outgrow our houses—our lease expires after so many years and then we shall want an entirely different class of furniture; consequently we purchase articles that have only sufficient life in them to last the brief

Of the Room and Furniture.

period of our occupation, and are content to abide by the want of appropriateness or beauty, in the clear intention of some day surrounding ourselves with objects that shall be joys to us for the remainder of our life. Another deterrent condition to making a serious outlay in furniture is the instability of fashion : each decade sees a new style, and the furniture that we have acquired in the exercise of our experienced taste will in all probability be discarded by the impetuous purism of the succeeding generation.

At present we are suffering from such a catholicity of taste as sees good in everything, and has an indifferent and tepid appreciation of all and sundry, especially if consecrated by age.

This is mainly a reaction against the austerity of those moralists who preached the logic of construction, and who required outward proof of the principles on which and by which each piece was designed.

Another cause prejudicial to the growth of modern furniture is the canonisation of old.

That tables and chairs should have lasted one hundred years is indeed proof that they were originally well made: that the conditions of the moment of their make were better than they are now is possible, and such aureole as is their due let us hasten to offer. But, to take advantage of their survival and to increase their number by facsimile reproduction is to paralyse all healthy growth of manufacture.

As an answer to the needs and habits of our ancestors of one hundred years ago—both in construction and design—let them serve us as models showing the attitude of mind in which we should meet the problems of our day—and so far as the needs and habits of the present time are unchanged, as models of form, not to be incorporated with our vernacular, but which we should recognise as successful form, and discover the plastic secrets of its shape.

With this possession we may borrow what forms we will—shapes of the Ind and far Cathay—the whole wide world is open to us—of past imaginations and of the dreams of our own.

But without this master-key the copying is slavish, and the bondage of the task is both cruel and destructive.

Cruel, because mindless, work can be reproduced more rapidly than thoughtful work can be invented, and the rate of production affects the price of other articles of similar kind, so that the one dictates what the other shall receive; and destructive, because it treats the craftsman as a mere machine, whose only standard can be mechanical excellence.

Now, all furniture that has any permanent value has been designed and wrought to meet the ends it had to serve, and the careful elaboration of it gave its maker scope for his pleasure and occasion for his pride.

If a man really likes what he has got to do, he will make great shifts to express and realise his pleasure ; he will choose carefully his materials, and either in playfulness of fancy, or in grave renunciation of the garniture of his art, will put the stamp of his individuality on his work.

An example of living art in modern furniture is a costermonger's barrow. Affectionately put together, carved and painted, it expresses almost in words the pride and taste of its owner.

As long as we are incapable of

recognising and sympathising with the delight of the workman in the realisation of his art, our admiration of his work is a pretence, and our encouragement of it blind—and this blindness makes us insensitive as to whether the delight is really there or no; consequently our patronage will most often be disastrous rather than helpful.

The value of furniture depends on the directness of its response to the requirements that called it into being, and to the nature of the conditions that evoked it.

To obtain good furniture we must contrive that the conditions of its service are worthy conditions, and not merely the dictates of our fancy or our sloth.

At the present moment modern furniture may be roughly divided into two classes: furniture for service, and furniture for display. Most of us, however, have to confine ourselves to the possession of serviceable furniture only; and a more frank recognition of this limitation would assist us greatly in our selection. If only we kept our real needs steadily before us, how much more beauty we could import into our homes!

Owing to lack of observation, and of experienced canons of taste, our fancies are caught by some chance object that pleases—one of that huge collection of ephemeral articles which "have been created to supply a want" that hitherto has never been felt—and as the cost of these fictions is (by the nature of the case) so low as to be of no great moment to us, the thing is purchased and helps henceforth to swell the museum of incongruous accumulation that goes by the name of a "furnished drawing-room."

A fancy, so caught, is soon outworn,

but the precept of economy forbids the discharge of the superfluous purchase, and so it adds its unit to the sum of daily labour spent on its preservation and its appearance. This burden of unnecessary toil is the index of the needlessness and cruelty with which we spend the labour of those whom need has put under our service.

And the sum of money spent on these ill-considered acquisitions which have gone to swell the general total of distress, an ever-widening ring of bitter ripple, might, concentrated, have purchased some one thing, both beautiful and useful, whose fashioning had been a pleasure to the artificer, and whose presence was an increasing delight to the owner and an added unit to this world's real wealth.

Such indiscriminate collection defeats its own aim. Compare the way Giovanni Bellini fits up St. Jerome's study for him in the National Gallery. There is no stint of money evidently; the Saint gets all that he can properly want, and he gets over and above—the addition born of his denial—the look of peace and calm in his room, that can so seldom be found with us. Another reason why our rooms are so glaringly over-furnished is, that many of us aim at a standard of profusion, in forgetfulness of the circumstances which created that standard. Families, whose descent has been historic, and whose home has been their pride, accumulate, in the lapse of time, heirlooms of many kinds—pictures, furniture, trinkets, etc.—and as these increase in numbers, the rooms in which they are contained become filled and crowded beyond what beauty or comfort permits, and such sacrifice is justly made for the demands of filial pride.

This emotion is so conspicuously an

honourable one that we are all eager to possess and give scope to our own, and so long as the scope is honest there is nothing more laudable.

But the temptation is to add to our uninherited display in this particular by substitutes, and to surround ourselves with immemorable articles, the justification of whose presence really should be that they form part of the history of our lives in more important respects than the mere occasions of their purchase.

It is this unreasoning ambition that leads to the rivalling of princely houses by the acquisition of "family portraits purchased in Wardour Street"—the rivalling of historic libraries by the purchase of thousands of books to form our yesterday's libraries of undisturbed volumes—the rivalling of memorable chairs and tables, by recently bought articles of our own, crowded in imitation of our model with innumerable trifles, to the infinite tax of our space, our patience, and our purse.

Our want of care and restraint in the selection of our furniture affects both its design and manufacture.

Constantly articles are bought for temporary use—we postponing the responsibility of wise purchase until we have more time, or else we buy what is not precisely what we want but which must do, since we cannot wait to have the exact things made, and have not the time to search elsewhere for them.

Furniture, in response to this demand, must be made either so striking as to arrest the eye, or so variedly serviceable as to meet some considerable proportion of the conflicting requirements made on it by the chance intending purchaser, or else it must fall back on the impregnable basis of antiquity and silence all argument with the canon that what the late Mr. Chippendale did was bound to be "good taste."

"There should be a place for everything, and everything in its place." Very true. But in the exercise of our orderliness we require the hearty co-operation of the "place" itself. 'Tis a wonderful aid when the place fits the object it is intended to contain.

Take the common male chest of drawers as a case in point. Its function is to hold a man's shirts and his clothes, articles of a known and constant size. Why are the drawers not made proportionate for their duty? Why are they so few and so deep that when filled—as they needs must be—they are uneasy to draw out, and to obtain the particular article of which we are in quest, and which of course is at the bottom, we must burrow into the heavy superincumbent mass of clothes in our search, and—that successful—spend a weary while in contriving to repack the ill-disposed space. It can hardly be economy of labour and material that dictates this, for—if so—why is the usual hanging wardrobe made so preposterously too tall? Does the idiot maker suppose that a woman's dress is hung all in one piece, body and skirt, from the nape of the neck, to trail its extremest length?

The art of buying furniture, or having it made for us, is to be acquired only by study and pains, and we must either pursue the necessary education, or depute the furnishing of our rooms to competent hands: and the responsibility does not end here, for there is the duty of discovering who are competent, and this must be done indirectly since direct inquiry only elicits the one criterion, omnipotent, omnipresent, of cost.

The object to be gained in furnishing a room is to supply the just requirements of the occupants, to accentuate or further the character of the room, and to indicate the individual habits and tastes of the owner.

Of the Room and Furniture.

Each piece should be beautiful in itself, and, still more important, should minister to and increase the beauty of the others. Collective beauty is to be aimed at; not so much individual.

Proportion is another essential. Not that the proportions of furniture should vary with the size of the rooms: the dimensions of chairs, height of tables, sizes of doors, have long been all fixed and, having direct reference to the human body, are immutable.

Substantially, the size of man's body is the same and has been the same from the dawn of history until now, and will be the same whether in a cottage parlour or the Albert Hall. But there is a proportion in the relations of the spaces of a room to its furniture which must be secured. If this is not done, no individual beauty of the objects in the room will repair the lost harmony or be compensation for the picture that might have been.

A museum of beautiful objects has its educational value, but no one pretends that it claims to be more than a storehouse of beauty.

The painter who crowds his canvas with the innumerable spots of colour that can be squeezed out of every tube of beautiful paint that the colourman sells, is no nearer his goal than he who fills his rooms with a heterogeneous miscellany of articles swept together from every clime and of every age.

Halsey Ricardo.

THE ENGLISH TRADITION

THE sense of a consecutive tradition has so completely faded out of English art that it has become difficult to realise the meaning of tradition, or the possibility of its ever again reviving; and this state of things is not improved by the fact that it is due to uncertainty of purpose, and not to any burning fever of individualism. Tradition in art is a matter of environment, of intellectual atmosphere. As the result of many generations of work along one continuous line, there has accumulated a certain amount of ability in design and manual dexterity, certain ideas are in the air, certain ways of doing things come to be recognised as the right ways. To all this endowment an artist born in any of the living ages of art succeeded as a matter of course, and it is the absence of this inherited knowledge that places the modern craftsman under exceptional disabilities.

There is evidence to prove the existence in England of hereditary crafts in which the son succeeded the father for generations, and to show that the guilds were rather the guardians of high traditional skill than mere trades unions; but there is surer proof of a common thread of tradition in certain qualities all along the line, which gave to English work a character peculiar to itself. Instances of genuine Gothic furniture are rare; in England at any rate it was usually simple and solid, sufficient to answer the needs of an age without any highly developed sense of the luxuries of life. It is not till the Renaissance that much material can be found for a history of English furniture. Much of the *motif* of this work came from Italy and the Netherlands; indeed cabinet work was imported largely from the latter country. It was just here, however, that tradition stepped in, and gave to our sixteenth and seventeenth century furniture a distinctly national character. The delicate mouldings, the skilful turnings, the quiet inlays of ebony, ivory, cherry wood, and walnut, above all the breadth and sobriety of its design, point to a tradition of craftsmanship strong enough to assimilate all the ideas which it borrowed from other ages and other countries. Contrast, for instance, a piece of Tottenham Court Road marquetry with the mother-of-pearl and ebony inlay on an English cabinet at South Kensington. So far as mere skill in cutting goes there may be no great difference between the two, but the latter is charming, and the former tedious in the last degree; and the reason is that in the seventeenth century the craftsman loved his work, and was master of it. He started with an idea in his head, and used his material with meaning, and so his inlay is as fanciful as the seaweed, and yet entirely subordinated to the harmony of the whole design. Perhaps some of the best furniture work ever done in England was done between 1600 and 1660. I refer, of course, to the good examples, to work which depended for its effect on refined design and delicate detail, not to the bulbous legs and coarse carving of ordinary Elizabethan, though even this had a *naïveté* and spontaneity entirely lacking in modern reproductions.

The English Tradition.

After the Restoration, signs of French influence appear in English furniture, but the tradition of structural fitness and dignity of design was preserved through the great architectural age of Wren and Gibbs, and lasted till the latter half of the eighteenth century. If that century was not particularly inspired, it at least understood consummate workmanship. The average of technical skill in the handicrafts was far in advance of the ordinary trade work of the present day. Some curious evidences of the activity prevailing in what are called the minor arts may be found in *The Laboratory and School of Arts*, a small octavo volume published in 1738. The work of this period furnishes a standing instance of the value of tradition. By the beginning of the eighteenth century a school of carvers had grown up in England who could carve, with absolute precision and without mechanical aids, all such ornament as egg and tongue work, or the acanthus, and other conventional foliage used for the decoration of the mouldings of doors, mantelpieces, and the like. Grinling Gibbons is usually named as the founder of this school, but Gibbons was himself trained by such men as Wren and Gibbs, and for the source from which this work derives the real stamp of style one must go back to the austere genius of Inigo Jones. The importance of the architect, in influencing craftsmen in all such matters as this, cannot be overrated. He has, or ought to have, sufficient knowledge of the crafts to settle for the craftsman the all-important points of scale and proportion to the rest of the design; and this is just one of those points in which contemporary architecture, both as regards the education of the architect and current practice, is exceedingly apt to fail. Sir William Chambers and the brothers Adam were the last of the architects before the cataclysm of the nineteenth century who made designs for furniture with any degree of skill.

The English Tradition.

In the latter half of the eighteenth century occur the familiar names of Chippendale, Heppelwhite, and Sheraton, and if these excellent cabinetmakers did a tenth of the work with which the dealers credit them, they must each have had the hundred hands of Gyas. The rosewood furniture inlaid with arabesques in thin flat brass, and made by Gillow at the end of the last century, is perhaps the last genuine effort in English furniture, though the tradition of good work and simple design died very hard in old-fashioned country places. The mischief began with the ridiculous mediævalism of Horace Walpole, which substituted amateur fancy for craftsmanship, and led in the following century to the complete extinction of any tradition whatever. The heavy attempts at furniture in the Greek style which accompanied the architecture of Wilkins and Soane were as artificial as this literary Gothic, and the two resulted in the chaos of art which found its expression in the great Exhibition of 1851.

Three great qualities stamped the English tradition in furniture so long as it was a living force—steadfastness of purpose, reserve in design, and thorough workmanship. Take any good period of English furniture, and one finds certain well-recognised types consistently adhered to throughout the country. There is no difficulty in grasping their general characteristics, whereas the very genius of classification could furnish no clue to the labyrinth of nineteenth-century design. The men of these earlier times made no laborious search for quaintness, no disordered attempt to combine the peculiarities of a dozen different ages. One general type was adhered to because it was the legacy of generations, and there was no reason for departing from such an excellent model. The designers and the workmen had only to perfect what was already good; they made no experiments in ornament, but used it with nice judgment, and full knowledge of its effect. The result was that, instead of being forced and unreasonable, their work was thoroughly happy; one cannot think of it as better done than it is.

The quality of reserve and sobriety is even more important. As compared with the later developments of the

The English Tradition.

Renaissance on the Continent, English furniture was always distinguished by its simplicity and self-restraint. Yet it is this very quality which is most conspicuously absent from modern work. As a people we rather pride ourselves on the resolute suppression of any florid display of feeling, but art in this country is so completely divorced from everyday existence, that it never seems to occur to an Englishman to import some of this fine insular quality into his daily surroundings.

It has been reserved for this generation to part company with the tradition of finished workmanship. Good work of course can be done, but it is exceedingly difficult to find the workman, and the average is bad. We have nothing to take the place of the admirable craftsmanship of the last century, which included not only great manual skill, but also an assured knowledge of the purpose of any given piece of furniture, of the form best suited for it, and the exact strength of material necessary, a knowledge which came of long familiarity with the difficulties of design and execution, which never hesitated in its technique, which attained a rightness of method so complete as to seem inevitable. Craftsmanship of this order hardly exists nowadays. It is the result of tradition, of the labour of many generations of cunning workmen.

Lastly, as the complement of these lapses on the part of the craftsman, there has been a gradual decadence in the taste of the public. Science and mechanical ingenuity have gone far to destroy the art of the handicrafts. Art is a matter of the imagination, and of the skill of one's hands—but the pace nowadays is too much for it. Certainly from the sixteenth to the eighteenth century a well-educated English gentleman had some knowledge of the arts, and especially of architecture; the Earl of Burlington even designed important buildings, though not with remarkable success; but at any rate educated people had some insight into the arts, whether inherited or acquired. Nowadays good education and breeding are no guarantee for anything of the sort, unless it is some miscellaneous knowledge of pictures. Few people, outside the artists, and not too many of them, give any serious attention to architecture and sculpture, and consequently an art such as furniture, which is based almost entirely upon these, is hardly recognised by the public as an art at all. How much the artist and his public react upon each other is shown by the plain fact that up to the last few years they have steadily marched down hill together, and it is not very certain that they have yet begun to turn the corner. That our English tradition was once a living thing is shown by the beautiful furniture, purely English in design and execution, still to be seen in great houses and museums, but it is not likely that such a tradition will spring up again till the artists try to make the unity of the arts a real thing, and the craftsman grows callous to fashion and archæology, and the public resolutely turns its back on what is tawdry and silly.

REGINALD BLOMFIELD.

CARPENTERS' FURNITURE

IT requires a far search to gather up examples of furniture really representative in this kind, and thus to gain a point of view for a prospect into the more ideal where furniture no longer is bought to look expensively useless in a boudoir, but serves everyday and commonplace need, such as must always be the wont, where most men work, and exchange in some sort life for life.

The best present-day example is the deal table in those last places to be vulgarised, farm-house or cottage kitchen. But in the Middle Ages things as simply made as a kitchen table, mere carpenters' framings, were decorated to the utmost stretch of the imagination by means simple and rude as their construction. Design, indeed, really fresh and penetrating, co-exists it seems only with simplest conditions.

Carpenters' Furniture.

Simple, serviceable movables fall into few kinds: the box, cupboard, and table, the stool, bench, and chair. The box was once the most frequent, useful, and beautiful of all these; now it is never made as furniture. Often it was seat, coffer, and table in one, with chequers inlaid on the top for chess. There are a great number of chests in England as early as the thirteenth century. One type of construction, perhaps the earliest, is to clamp the wood-work together and beautifully decorate it by branching scrolls of iron-work. Another kind was ornamented

Carpenters' Furniture.

by a sort of butter-print patterning, cut into the wood in ingenious fillings to squares and circles, which you can imitate by drawing the intersecting lines the compasses seem to make of their own will in a circle, and cutting down each space to a shallow V. This simple carpenter's decoration is especially identified with chests. The same kind of work is still done in Iceland and Norway, the separate compartments often brightly painted into a mosaic of colour; or patterns of simple scroll-work are made out in incised line and space. In Italy this charming art of incising was carried much farther in the *cassoni*, the fronts of which, broad planks of cypress wood, are often romantic with quite a tapestry of kings and ladies, beasts, birds, and foliage, cut in outline with a knife and punched with dots,

Carpenters' Furniture.

the cavities being filled with a coloured mastic like sealing-wax. Panelling, rough inlaying in the solid, carving and painting, and casing with repoussé or pierced metal, or covering with leather incised into designs, and making out patterns with nail-heads, were all methods of decoration used by the maker of boxes: other examples, and those not the least stately, had no other ornament than the purfling at the edges formed by ingeniously elaborate dovetails fitting together like a puzzle and showing a pattern like an inlay.

When people work naturally, it is as wearisome and unnecessary often to repeat the same design as to continually paint the same picture. Design comes by designing. On the one hand tradition carefully and continuously shapes the object to fill its use, on the other spontaneous and eager excursions are made

Carpenters' Furniture.

into the limitless fields of beautiful device. Where construction and form are thus the result of a long tradition undisturbed by fashion, they are always absolutely right as to use and distinctive as to beauty, the construction being not only visible, but one with the decoration. Take a present-day survival, the large country cart, the body shaped like the waist of a sailing ship, and every rail and upright unalterably logical, and then decorated by quaint chamferings, the facets of which are made out in brightest paint. Or look at an old table, always with stretching rails at the bottom and framed together with strong tenons and cross pins into turned posts, but so thoughtfully done that every one is original and all beautiful. Turning, a delightful old art, half for convenience, half for beauty, itself comes down to us from long before the Conquest.

The great charm in furniture of the simplest structure may best be seen in old illuminated manuscripts, where a chest, a bench, and against the wall a cupboard, the top rising in steps where are set out tall "Venice glasses," or a "garnish" of plate under a tester of some bright stuff, make up a whole of fairy beauty in the frank simplicity of the forms and the innocent gaiety of bright colour. Take the St. Jerome in his study of Dürer or Bellini, and compare the dignity of serene and satisfying order with the most beautifully furnished room you know: how vulgar our *good taste* appears and how foreign to the end of culture—Peace.

Carpenters' Furniture.

From records, and what remains to us, we know that the room, the hangings, and the furniture were patterned all over with scattered flowers and inscriptions—violets and the words "*bonne pensée*";

Carpenters' Furniture.

or vases of lilies and "pax," angels and incense pots, ciphers and initials, badges and devices, or whatever there be of suggestion and mystery. The panelling and furniture were "green like a curtain," as the old accounts have it; or vermilion and white, like some painted chairs at Knole; or even decorated with paintings and gilt gesso patterns like the Norfolk screens. Fancy a bed with the underside of the canopy having an Annunciation or spreading trellis of roses, and the chamber carved like one in thirteenth-century romance:—

"N'a el monde beste n'oisel
Qui n'i soit ovré à cisel."

If we would know how far we are from the soul of art, we have but to remember that all this, the romance element in design, the joy in life, nature, and colour, which in one past development we call Gothic, and which is ever the well of beauty undefiled, is not now so much impossible of attainment as entirely out of range with our spirit and life, a felt anachronism and affectation.

Carpenters' Furniture.

All art is sentiment embodied in form. To find beauty we must consider what really gives us pleasure—pleasure, not pride—and show our unashamed delight in it; "and so, when we have leisure to be happy and strength to be simple we shall find Art again"—the art of the workman.

W. R. Lethaby.

OF DECORATED FURNITURE

DECORATED or "sumptuous" furniture is not merely furniture that is expensive to buy, but that which has been elaborated with much thought, knowledge, and skill. Such furniture cannot be cheap, certainly, but the real cost of it is sometimes borne by the artist who produces rather than by the man who may happen to buy it. Furniture on which valuable labour is bestowed may consist of—1. Large standing objects which, though actually movable, are practically fixtures, such as cabinets, presses, sideboards of various kinds;

monumental objects. 2. Chairs, tables of convenient shapes, stands for lights and other purposes, coffers, caskets, mirror and picture frames. 3. Numberless small convenient utensils. Here we can but notice class 1, the large standing objects which most absorb the energies of artists of every degree and order in their construction or decoration.

Cabinets seem to have been so named as being little strongholds—"offices" of men of business for stowing papers and documents in orderly receptacles. They are secured with the best locks procurable. They often contain secret drawers and cavities, hidden from all eyes but those of the owner. Nor are instances wanting of owners leaving no information on these matters to their heirs, so that casual buyers sometimes come in for a windfall, or such a catastrophe as befell the owner of Richard the Third's bed.

It is not to be expected that elaborate systems of secret drawers and hiding-places should be contrived in cabinets of our time. Money and jewels are considered safer when deposited in banks. But, ingenuity of construction in a complicated piece of furniture must certainly be counted as one of its perfections. Sound and accurate joinery with well-seasoned woods, properly understood as to shrinkage and as to the relations between one kind of timber and another in these respects, is no small merit.

Some old English cabinets are to be met with in the construction of which wood only is used, the morticing admirable, the boards, used to hold ends and divisions together from end to end, strained and secured by wedges that turn on pivots, etc. Furniture of this kind can be taken to pieces and set up, resuming proper rigidity *toties quoties.*

To look at the subject historically, it seems that the cabinet, dresser, or side-board is a chest set on legs, and that the "press," or cupboard (closet, not proper *cup*-board), takes the place of the panelled recess closed by doors, generally contrived, and sometimes ingeniously hidden, in the construction of a panelled room. The front of the elevated chest is hinged, and flaps down, while the lid is a fixture; the interior is more complicated than that of the chest, as its subdivisions are more conveniently reached.

Before leaving this part of the subject, it is worth notice that the architectural, or rather architectonic, character seems to have deeply impressed the makers of cabinets when the chest-type had gradually been lost. Italian, German, English,

Of Decorated Furniture.

and other cabinets are often found representing a church front or a house front, with columns, doors, sometimes ebony and ivory pavements, etc.

Next as to methods of decorating cabinets, etc. The kind which deserves our first attention is that of sculpture. Here, undoubtedly, we must look to the Italians as our masters, and to that admirable school of wood-carving which maintained itself so long in Flanders, with an Italian grace grafted on the ingenuity, vigour, and playfulness of a northern race. Our English carvers, admirable craftsmen during the fifteenth and sixteenth centuries, seem to have been closely allied with the contemporary Flemings. Fronts of cabinets, dressers, chimney-pieces, etc., were imported from Belgium and were made up by English joiners with panelling, supplemented with carving where required, for our great houses.

But the best Italian carving remains on chests and chest fronts which were made in great numbers in the sixteenth century.

Some of these chests are toilet chests; some have formed wall-seats, laid along the sides of halls and galleries to hold hangings, etc., when the house was empty, and have served as seats or as "monumental" pieces when company was received.

As the chest grew into the cabinet, or bureau, or dresser, great attention was paid to the supports. It need hardly be pointed out that, for the support of seats, tables, etc., animals, typical of strength or other qualities—the lion or the sphinx, the horse, sometimes the slave—have been employed by long traditional usage. And carvers of wood have not failed to give full attention to the use and decoration of conventional supports to the furniture now under discussion. They are made to unite the central mass to a shallow base, leaving the remaining space open.

Next to sculptured decoration comes incrusted. The most costly kinds of material, precious stones, such as lapis lazuli, agate, rare marbles, etc., have been employed on furniture surfaces. But such work is rather that of the lapidary than of the cabinetmaker. It is very costly, and seems to have been confined, in fact, to the factories kept up in Italy, Russia, and other states, at government expense. We do not produce them in this country; and the number of such objects is probably limited wherever we look for them.

Incrustation of precious woods is a more natural system of wood-decoration. Veneered wood, which is laid on a roughened surface with thin glue at immense pressure, if well made, is very long-lived. The woods used give a coloured surface, and are polished so as to bring the colour fully out, *and* to protect the material from damp. In fine examples the veneers form little pictures, or patterns, either by the arrangement of the grain of the pieces used, so as to make pictorial lines by means of the grain itself, or by using woods of various colours.

A very fine surface decoration was invented, or carried to perfection, by André Charles Boule, for Louis XIV. It is a veneer of tortoise-shell and brass, with occasional white metal. An important element in Boule decoration is noticeable in the chiselled angle mounts, lines of moulding, claws, feet, etc., all of which are imposed, though they have the general character of metal angle supports. In fact, the tortoise-shell is held by glue, and the metal by fine nails of the same material, the heads of which are filed down. Incrustation, or *marquetry*, of this kind is costly, and most of it is due to the labours of artists and craftsmen employed by the kings of France at the expense of the Government. A considerable quantity of it is still made in that country.

Now as to the way in which sculptors, or incrusters, should dispose of their decoration, and the fidelity to nature which is to be expected of them, whether in sculpture or wood mosaic, *i.e.* wood painting. First, we may suppose they will concentrate their more important details in recognisable divisions of their pieces, or in such ways that a proportion and rhythm shall be expressed by their dispositions of masses and fine details; placing their figures in central panels, on angles, or on dividing members; leaving some plain surface to set off their decorative detail; and taking care that the contours of running mouldings shall not be lost sight of by the carver. But how far is absolute natural truth, even absolute obedience to the laws of his art in every particular of his details, to be expected from the artist? We cannot doubt that such absolute obedience is sometimes departed from intentionally and with success. All Greek sculpture is not always absolutely true to nature nor as beautiful as the sculptor, if free, could have made it. Statues are conventionalised, decorative scrolls exaggerated, figures turned into columns for good reasons, and in the result successfully. In furniture, as in architecture, carved work or incrustation is not *free*, but is in *service*; and compromises with verisimilitude to nature, even violence, may sometimes be required on details in the interests of the entire structure.

Of Decorated Furniture.

Next let a word or two be reserved for Painted Furniture. Painting has been employed on furniture of all kinds at many periods. The ancients made theirs of bronze, or of ivory, carved or inlaid. In the Middle Ages wood-carving and many kinds of furniture were painted. The coronation chair at Westminster was so decorated. The chest fronts of Delli and other painters are often pictures of great intrinsic merit, and very generally these family chest fronts are valuable records of costumes and fashions of their day. In this country the practice of painting pianoforte cases, chair-backs, table-tops, panels of all sorts, has been much resorted to. Distinguished painters, Angelica Kauffmann and her contemporaries, and a whole race of coach-painters have left monuments of their skill in this line. It must suffice here to recall certain modern examples, *e.g.*

a small dresser, now in the national collections, with doors painted by Mr. Poynter, with spirited figures representing the *Beers* and the *Wines*; the fine piano case painted by Mr. Burne-Jones; another by Mr. Alma Tadema; lastly, a tall clock-case by Mr. Stanhope, which, as well as other promising examples, have been exhibited by the Arts and Crafts Society.

Of Decorated Furniture.

J. H. Pollen.

OF CARVING

IT is not uncommon to see an elaborate piece of furniture, in decorating which it is evident that the carver has had opportunity for the exercise of all his skill, and which, indeed, bears evidence of the most skilful woodcutting on almost every square inch of its surface, from the contemplation of which neither an artist nor an educated craftsman can derive any pleasure or satisfaction. This would seem to point to the designer of the ornament as the cause of failure, and the writer of this believes that in such cases it will generally be found that the designer, though he may know everything that he ought to know about the production of designs which shall look well on paper or on a flat surface, has had no experience, by actually working at the material, of its difficulties, special capabilities, or limitations.

If at the same time he has had but a limited experience of the difference in treatment necessary for carving which is to be seen at various altitudes, his failure may be taken as sufficiently accounted for.

An idea now prevalent that it is not advisable to make models for woodcarving is not by any means borne out by the experience of the writer of this paper.

Models are certainly not necessary for ordinary work, such as mouldings, or even for work in panels when the surfaces are intended to be almost wholly on one plane, but the carved decoration of a panel, which pretends to be in any degree a work of art, often depends for its effect quite as much on the masterly treatment of surface planes, and the relative projection from the surface of the more prominent parts, as upon the outline. Now, there are many men who, though able to carve wood exquisitely, have never given themselves the trouble, or perhaps have scarcely had the opportunity, to learn how to read an ordinary drawing. The practice obtains in many carving shops for one or two leading men to rough out (*viz.* shape out roughly) all the work so far as that is practicable, and the others take it up after them and finish it. The followers are not necessarily less skilful carvers or cutters than the leaders, but have, presumably, less knowledge of form. If, then, one wishes to avail oneself of the skill of these men for carrying out really important work, it is much the simpler way to make a model (however rough) which shall accurately express everything one wishes to see in the finished work; and, assuming the designer to be fairly dexterous in the use of clay or other plastic material, a sketch model will not occupy any more of his time than a drawing would.

To put it plainly, no designer can ever know what he ought to expect from a worker in any material if he has not worked in that material himself. If he has carved marble, for instance, he knows the extreme care required in undercutting the projecting parts of the design, and the cost entailed by the processes necessary to be employed for that purpose. He therefore so arranges the various parts of his design that wherever it is possible these projecting portions shall be supported by other forms, so avoiding

Of Carving. the labour and cost of relieving (or under-cutting) them ; and if he be skilful his skill will appear in the fact that his motive in this will be apparent only to experts, while to others the whole will appear to grow naturally out of the design. Moreover, he knows that he must depend for the success of this thing on an effect of breadth and dignity. He is not afraid of a somewhat elaborate surface treatment, being aware that nearly any variety of surface which he can readily produce in clay may be rendered in marble with a reasonable amount of trouble.

In designing for the wood-carver he is on altogether different ground. He may safely lay aside some portion of his late dignity, and depend almost entirely on vigour of line; the ease with which under-cutting is done in this material enabling him to obtain contrast by the use of delicately relieved forms. Here, however, he must not allow the effect in his model to depend in any degree on surface treatment. Care in that respect will prevent disappointment in the finished work.

The most noticeable feature in modern carved surface decoration is the almost universal tendency to overcrowding. It appears seldom to have occurred to the craftsman or designer that decorating a panel, for instance, is not at all the same thing as covering it with decoration. Still less does he seem to have felt that occasionally some portions of the ground are much more valuable in the design than anything which he can put on them. Indeed, the thoughtful designer who understands its use and appreciates its value, frequently has more trouble with his ground than with anything else in the panel. Also, if he have the true decorative spirit, his mind is constantly on the general scheme surrounding his work, and he is always ready to subordinate himself and his work in order that it may enhance and not disturb this general scheme.

We will suppose, for example, that he has to decorate a column with raised ornament. He feels at once that the outlines of that column are of infinitely more importance than anything which he can put on it, however ingenious or beautiful his design may be. He therefore keeps his necessary projecting parts as small and low as possible, leaving as much of the column as he can showing between the lines of his pattern. By this means the idea of strength and support is not interfered with, and the *tout ensemble* is not destroyed.

This may seem somewhat elementary to many who will read it. My excuse must be that one sees many columns in which every vestige of the outline is so covered by the carving which has been built round them, that the idea of their supporting anything other than their ornament appears preposterous.

There has been no opportunity to do more than glance at such a subject as this in a space so limited; but the purposes of this paper will have been served if it has supplied a useful hint to any craftsman, or if by its means any designer shall have been induced to make a more thorough study of the materials within his reach.

STEPHEN WEBB.

INTARSIA AND INLAID WOOD-WORK

ALTHOUGH decoration by inlaying woods of different colours must naturally have suggested itself in very early times, as soon indeed as there were workmen of skill sufficient for it, the history of this branch of art practically begins in the fifteenth century. It is eminently an Italian art, which according to Vasari had its origin in the days of Brunelleschi and Paolo Uccello; and it had its birth in a land which has a greater variety of mild close-grained woods with a greater variety of colour than Northern Europe. By the Italians it was regarded as a lower form of painting. Like all mosaic, of which art it is properly a branch, it has its limitations; and it is only so long as it confines itself to these that it is a legitimate form of decoration. Tarsia is at the best one of the minor decorative arts, but when well employed it is one that gives an immense deal of pleasure, and one to which it cannot be denied that the buildings of Italy owe much of their splendour. Their polished and inlaid furniture harmonises with the rare delicacy of their marble and mosaic, and goes far towards producing that air of rich refinement and elaborate culture which is to the severer styles and simpler materials of the North what the velvet-robed Senator of St. Mark was to the mail-clad feudal chief from beyond the Alps. As to its durability, the experience of four

Intarsia and Inlaid Wood-work.

centuries since Vasari's time has proved that with ordinary care, or perhaps with nothing worse than mere neglect, Intarsia will last as long as painting. Its only real enemy is damp, as will be readily understood from the nature of the materials and the mode of putting them together. For though in a few instances, when the art was in its infancy, the inlaid pattern may have been cut of a substantial thickness and sunk into a solid ground ploughed out to receive it, this method was obviously very laborious, and admitted only of very simple design, for it is very difficult in this way to keep the lines of the drawing accurately. The recognised way of making Intarsia was, and is, to form both pattern and ground in thin veneers about $\frac{1}{16}$ of an inch thick, which are glued down upon a solid panel. At first sight this method may appear too slight and unsubstantial for work intended to last for centuries, but it has, in fact, stood the test of time extremely well, when the work has been kept in the dry even temperature of churches and great houses, where there is neither damp to melt the glue and swell the veneer, nor excessive heat to make the wood shrink and start asunder. When these conditions were not observed, of course the work was soon ruined, and Vasari tells an amusing story of the humiliation which befell Benedetto da Majano, who began his career as an *Intarsiatore*, in the matter of two splendid chests which he had made for Matthias Corvinus, from which the veneers, loosened by the damp of a sea voyage, fell off in the royal presence.

The veneers being so thin, it is of course easy to cut through several layers of them at once, and this suggested, or at all events lent itself admirably to the

Intarsia and Inlaid Wood-work.

design of the earlier examples, which are generally arabesques symmetrically disposed right and left of a central line. If two dark and two light veneers are put together, the whole of one panel, both ground and pattern, can be cut at one operation with a thin fret saw; the ornamental pattern drops into the space cut out of the ground, which it, of course, fits exactly except for the thickness of the saw-cut, and the two half-patterns thus filled in are "handed" right and left, and so complete the symmetrical design. The line given by the thickness of the saw is then filled in with glue and black colour so as to define the outline, and additional saw-cuts are made or lines are engraved, and in either case filled in with the same stopping, wherever additional lines are wanted for the design. It only remains to glue the whole down to a solid panel, and to polish and varnish the surface, and it is then ready to be framed into its place as the back of a church stall, or the lining of a courtly hall, library, or cabinet.

Intarsia and Inlaid Wood-work.

It was thus that the simpler Italian Intarsia was done, such as that in the dado surrounding Perugino's Sala del Cambio in his native city, where the design consists of light arabesques in box or some similar wood on a walnut ground, defined by black lines just as I have described.

But like all true artists the Intarsiatore did not stand still. Having successfully accomplished simple outline and accurate drawing, he was dissatisfied until he could carry his art farther by introducing the refinement of shading. This was done at different times and by different artists in a variety of ways; either by inlaying the shadow in different kinds of woods, by scorching it with fire, or by staining it with chemical solutions. In the book desks of the choir at the Certosa or Charterhouse of Pavia, the effect of shading is got in a direct but somewhat imperfect way by laying strips of different coloured woods side by side. Each flower or leaf was probably built up of tolerably thick pieces of wood glued together in position, so that they could be sliced off in veneers and yield several flowers or leaves from the same block, much in the way of Tunbridge Wells ware, though the Italian specimens are, I believe, always cut *with* the grain and not across it. The designs thus produced are very effective at a short distance, but the method is, of course, suitable only to bold and simple conventional patterns.

The panels of the high screen or back to the stalls at the same church afford an instance of a more elaborate method. These splendid panels, which go all round the choir, contain each a three-quarter-length figure of a saint. Lanzi deservedly praises them as the largest and most perfect figures of *tarsia* which he had seen. They date from 1486, and were executed by an Istrian artist, Bartolommeo da Pola, perhaps from the designs of Borgognone. The method by which their highly pictorial effect is produced is a mixed one, the shading being partly inlaid with woods of different colours, and partly obtained by scorching the wood with fire or hot sand in the manner generally in use for marqueterie at the present day. The inexhaustible patience as well as the fertility of resource displayed by Messer Bartolommeo is astonishing. Where the saw-cut did not give him a strong enough line he has inlaid a firm line of black wood, the high

Intarsia and Inlaid Wood-work.

lights of the draperies are inlaid in white, the folds shaded by burning, and the flowing lines of the curling hair are all inlaid, each several tress being shaded by three narrow strips of gradated colour following the curved lines of the lock to which they belong. When it is remembered that there are some forty or more of these panels, each differing from the rest, the splendour as well as the laborious nature of the decoration of this unrivalled choir will be better understood.

Of all the examples of pictorial Intarsia the most elaborate are perhaps those in the choir stalls of Sta. Maria Maggiore in Bergamo. They are attributed to Gianfrancesco Capo di Ferro, who worked from the designs of Lotto, and was either a rival or pupil of Fra Damiano di Bergamo, a famous master of the art. They consist of figure subjects and

Intarsia and Inlaid Wood-work.

landscapes on a small scale, shaded with all the delicacy and roundness attainable in a tinted drawing, and certainly show how near Intarsia can approach to painting. Their drawing is excellent and their execution marvellous; but at the same time one feels that, however one may admire them as a *tour de force*, the limitations of good sense and proper use of the material have been reached and overstepped. When the delicacy of the work is so great that it requires to be covered up or kept under glass, it obviously quits the province of decorative art; furniture is meant to be used, and when it is too precious to be usable on account of the over-delicate ornament bestowed upon it, it must be admitted that the ornament is out of place, and, therefore, bad art.

The later Italian Intarsia was betrayed into extravagance by the dexterity of the craftsman. The temptation before which he fell was that of rivalling the painter, and as he advanced in facility of technique, and found wider resources at his command, he threw aside not only those restraints which necessity had hitherto imposed, but also those which good taste and judgment still called him to obey. In the plain unshaded arabesques of the Sala del Cambio, and even in the figure panels of the Certosa, the treatment is purely decorative; the idea of a plane surface is rightly observed, and there is no attempt to represent distance or to produce illusory effects of relief. Above all, the work is solid and simple enough to bear handling; the stalls may be sat in, the desks may be used for books, the doors may be opened and shut, without fear of injury to their decoration. Working within these limits, the art was safe; but they came in time to be disregarded, and in this, as in other branches of art, the style was ruined by the over-ingenuity of the artists. Conscious of their own dexterity, they attempted things never done before, with means quite unsuited to the purpose, and with the sole result that they did imperfectly and laboriously with their wooden veneers, their glue-pot, and their chemicals, what the painter did with crayon and brush perfectly and easily. Their greatest triumphs after they began to run riot in this way, however interesting as miracles of dexterity, have no value as works of art in the eyes of those who know the true principles of decorative design; while nothing can be much duller than the elaborate playfulness of the Intarsiatore who loved to cover his panelling with sham book-cases, birds in cages, guitars, and military instruments in elaborate perspective.

Intarsia and Inlaid Wood-work.

It would take too long to say much about the art in its application to furniture, such as tables, chairs, cabinets, and other movables, which are decorated with inlay that generally goes by the French name of marqueterie. Marqueterie and Intarsia are the same thing, though from habit the French title is generally used when speaking of work on a smaller scale. And as the methods and materials are the same, whether used on a grand or a small scale, so the same rules and restraints apply to both classes of design, and can no more be infringed with impunity on the door of a tall clock-case than on the doors of a palatial hall of audience. Nothing can be a prettier or more practical and durable mode of decorating furniture than marqueterie in simple brown, black, yellow, and white; and when used with judgment there is nothing to forbid the employment of dyed woods; while the smallness of the scale puts at our disposal ivory, mother-of-pearl, and tortoise-shell, materials which in larger works are naturally out of the question. Nothing, on the other hand, is more offensive to good taste than some of the overdone marqueterie of the French school of the last century, with its picture panels, and naturalesque figures, flowers, and foliage, straggling all over the surface, as if the article of furniture were merely a vehicle for the cleverness of the marqueterie cutter. Still worse is the modern work of the kind, whether English or foreign, of which so much that is hopelessly pretentious and vulgar is turned out now-adays, in which the aim of the designer seems to have been to cover the surface as thickly as he could with flowers and festoons of all conceivable colours, without any regard for the form of the thing

Intarsia and Inlaid Wood-work.

he was decorating, the nature of the material he was using, or the graceful disposition and economy of the ornament he was contriving.

T. G. Jackson.

WOODS AND OTHER MATERIALS

THE woods in ordinary use by cabinet-makers may be divided broadly into two classes, viz. those which by their strength, toughness, and other qualities are suitable for construction, and those which by reason of the beauty of their texture or grain, their rarity, or their costliness, have come to be used chiefly for decorative purposes—veneering or inlaying. There are certainly several woods which combine the qualities necessary for either purpose, as will be noticed later on. At present the

Woods and other Materials.

above classification is sufficiently accurate for the purposes of this paper. The woods chiefly used in the construction of cabinet work and furniture are oak, walnut, mahogany, rosewood, satin-wood, cedar, plane, sycamore.

The oak has been made the standard by which to measure all other woods for the qualities of strength, toughness, and durability. There are said to be nearly fifty species of oak known, but the common English oak possesses these qualities in a far greater degree than any other wood. It is, however, very cross-grained and difficult to manage where delicate details are required, and its qualities recommend it to the carpenter rather than to the furniture-maker, who prefers the softer and straight-grained oak from Turkey or wainscot from Holland, which, in addition to being more easily worked and taking a higher finish, is not so liable to warp or split.

There is also a species called white oak, which is imported into this country from America, and is largely used for interior fittings and cabinet-making. It is not equal to the British oak in strength or durability, and it is inferior to the wainscot in the beauty of its markings. The better the quality of this oak, the more it shrinks in drying.

Walnut is a favourite wood with the furniture-maker, as well as the carver, on account of its even texture and straight grain. The English variety is of a light grayish-brown colour, which colour improves much by age under polish. That from Italy has more gray in it, and though it looks extremely well when carved is less liked by carvers on account of its brittleness. It is but little liable to the attacks of worms. In the English

Woods and other Materials.

kind, the older (and therefore, generally speaking, the better) wood may be recognised by its darker colour.

Of mahogany there are two kinds, viz. those which are grown in the islands of Cuba and Jamaica, and in Honduras. The Cuba or Spanish mahogany is much the harder and more durable, and is, in the opinion of the writer, the very best wood for all the purposes of the cabinet or furniture maker known to us. It is beautifully figured, takes a fine polish, is not difficult to work, when its extreme hardness is taken into account, and is less subject to twisting and warping than any other kind of wood. It has become so costly of late years, however, that it is mostly cut into veneers, and used for the decoration of furniture surfaces.

Honduras mahogany, or, as cabinet-makers call it, "Bay Wood," is that which is now in most frequent demand for the construction of the best kinds of furniture and cabinet work. It is fairly strong (though it cannot compare in that respect with Cuba or rosewood), works easily, does not shrink, resists changes of temperature without alteration, and holds glue well, all of which qualities specially recommend it for the purposes of construction where veneers are to be used. Many cabinetmakers prefer to use this wood for drawers, even in an oak job.

Rosewood is one of those woods used indifferently for construction or for the decoration of other woods. Though beautiful specimens of grain and figure are often seen, its colour does not compare with good specimens of Cuba veneer. Its purple tone (whatever stains are used) is not so agreeable as the rich, deep, mellow browns of the mahogany; nor does it harmonise so readily with its surroundings in an ordinary room. It has great strength and durability, and is not difficult to work. Probably the best way to use it constructively is in the making of small cabinets, chairs, etc.—that is, if one wishes for an appearance of lightness with real strength. The writer does not here offer any opinion as to whether a piece of furniture, or indeed anything else, should or should not look strong when it really is so.

Satin-wood, most of which comes from the West India islands, is well known for its fine lustre and grain, as also for its warm colour, which is usually deepened by yellow stain. It is much used for painted furniture, and the plain variety is liked by the carver.

Cedar is too well known to need any description here. It is commonly believed that no worm will touch it, and it is therefore greatly in demand for the interior fitting of cabinets, drawers, etc. It is a straight-grained wood and fairly easy to work, though liable to split. It is impossible in a short paper like the present to do more than glance at a few of the numerous other woods in common use. Ebony has always been greatly liked for small or elaborate caskets or cabinets, its extreme closeness of grain and hardness enabling the carver to bring up the smallest details with all the sharpness of metal work.

Woods and other Materials.

Sycamore, beech, and holly are frequently stained to imitate walnut, rosewood, or other materials; of these the first two are used constructively, but the latter, which takes the stain best, is nearly all cut into veneer, and, in addition to its use for covering large surfaces, forms an important element in the modern marquetry decorations.

Bass wood, on account of its softness and the facility with which it can be stained to any requisite shade, is extensively used to imitate other woods in modern furniture of the cheaper sort. It should, however, never be used for furniture at all, as it has (as a cabinet-maker would say) no "nature" in it, and in the result there is no wear in it.

Other woods, coming under the second category, as amboyna, coromandel, snake-wood, orange-wood, thuyer, are all woods of a beautiful figure, which may be varied indefinitely by cutting the veneers at different angles to the grain of the wood, and the tone may also be varied by the introduction of colour into the polish which is used on them. Coromandel wood is one of the most beautiful of these, but it is not so available as it would otherwise be on account of its resistance to glue. Orange-wood, when not stained, is very wasteful in use, as the natural colour is confined to the heart of the tree.

Silver, white metal, brass, etc., are cut into a veneer of tortoise-shell or mother-of-pearl, producing a decorative effect which, in the opinion of the writer, is more accurately described as "gorgeous" than "beautiful."

Woods and other Materials.

There are many processes and materials used to alter or modify the colour of woods and to "convert" one wood into another. Oak is made dark by being subjected to the fumes of liquid ammonia, which penetrate it to almost any depth. Ordinary oak is made into brown oak by being treated with a solution of chromate of potash (which is also used to convert various light woods into mahogany, etc.). Pearlash is used for the same purpose, though not commonly. For converting pear-tree, sycamore, etc., into ebony, two or more applications of logwood chips, with an after application of vinegar and steel filings, are used.

Woods and other Materials.

A good deal of bedroom and other furniture is enamelled, and here the ground is prepared with size and whiting, and this is worked over with flake white, transparent polish, and bismuth. But by far the most beautiful surface treatment in this kind are the lacquers, composed of spirit and various gums, or of shellac and spirit into which colour is introduced.

STEPHEN WEBB.

OF MODERN EMBROIDERY

IF we wish to arrive at a true estimate of the value of modern embroidery, we must examine the work being sold in the fancy-work shops, illustrated in ladies' newspapers or embroidered in the drawing-rooms of to-day, and consider in what respect it differs from the old work such as that exhibited in the South Kensington Museum.

The old embroidery and the modern differ widely—in design, in colour, and in material; nor would any one deny that a very large proportion of modern work is greatly inferior to that of past times.

Of Modern Embroidery.

What, then, are the special characteristics of the design of the present day?

Modern design is frequently very naturalistic, and seems rather to seek after a life-like rendering of the object to be embroidered than the decoration of the material to be ornamented.

Then again it may be noted that modern designs are often ill adapted to the requirements of embroidery. This is probably because many of the people who design for embroidery do not understand it. Very often a design that has been made for this purpose would have been better suited to a wall paper, a panel of tiles, or a woven pattern The designer should either be also an embroiderer or have studied the subject so thoroughly as to be able to direct the worker, for the design should be drawn in relation to the colours and stitches in which it is to be carried out.

The more, indeed, people will study the fine designs of the past, and compare with them the designs of the art-needle-work of the present, the more they will realise that, where the former is rich, dignified, and restrained, obedient to law in every curve and line, the latter is florid, careless, weak, and ignores law. And how finished that old embroidery was, and how full! No grudging of the time or the labour spent either on design or needle-work; no scamping; no mere outlining. Border within border we often see, and all the space within covered up to the edges and into the corners. Contrast with this very much of our modern work. Let us take as an example one piece that was on view this summer at a well-known place in London where embroidery is sold. It is merely a type of many others in many other places. This was a three-fold screen made of dark red-brown velveteen. All over it ran diagonal crossing lines coarsely worked in light silk, to imitate a wire trellis, with occasional upright supports worked in brown wool, imitating knotty sticks. Up one side of this trellis climbed a scrambling mass of white clematis; one spray wandering along the top fell a little way down the other side. Thus a good part of the screen was bare of embroidery, except for the trellis. Naturalism could not go much farther, design is almost absent, and the result is feeble and devoid of beauty.

If we turn now to material, we shall find that embroidery, like some other arts, depends much for its excellence on the minor crafts which provide it with material; and these crafts supplied it with better material in former times than they do now. A stuff to be used as a ground for embroidery should have endless capacities for wear. This was a quality eminently possessed by hand-spun and hand-woven linen, which, with its rounded and separate thread, and the creamy tint of its partial bleaching, made an ideal ground for embroidery. Or if silk were preferred, the silks of past centuries were at once thick, firm, soft and pure, quite free from the dress or artificial thickening, by whose aid a silk nowadays tries to look rich when it is not. The oatmeal cloth, diagonal cloth, cotton-backed satin, velveteen and plush, so much used now, are very inferior materials as grounds for needle-work to the hand-loom linens and silks on which so large a part of the old embroidery remaining to us was worked. And so very much of the beauty of the embroidery depends on the appropriateness of the material.[1] Cloth, serge, and plush are not appropriate; embroidery

[1] But cf. "Of Materials," p. 365.

never looks half so well on them as on silk and linen.

It is equally important that the thread, whether of silk, wool, flax, or metal, should be pure and as well made as it can be, and, if dyed, dyed with colours that will stand light and washing. Most of the silk, wool, and flax thread sold for embroidery is not as good as it should be. The filoselles and crewels very soon get worn away from the surface of the material they are worked on. The crewels are made of too soft a wool, and are not twisted tight enough, and the filoselles, not being made of pure silk, should never be used at all, pretty and soft though their effect undoubtedly is while fresh. Though every imaginable shade of colour can be produced by modern dyers, the craft seems to have been better understood by the dyers of times not very long past, who, though they may not have been able to produce so many shades, could dye colours which would wash and did not quickly fade, or when they faded merely lost some colour, instead of changing colour, as so many modern dyes do. The old embroidery is worked with purer and fewer colours; now all kinds of dull intermediate tints are used of gold, brown, olive, and the like, which generally fade rapidly and will not wash. Many people, admiring old embroidery and desiring to make their new work look like it at least in colour, will use tints as faint and delicate as the faded old colours, forgetting that in a few years their work will be almost colourless. It is wiser to use strong good colours, for a little fading does not spoil but really improves them.

So we see that many things combine to render embroidery as fine as that of the past difficult of production, and there is nothing more against it than machinery, which floods the market with its cheap imitations, so that an embroidered dress is no longer the choice and rare production it once was; the machine-made imitation is so common and so cheap that a refined taste, sick of the vulgarity of the imitation, cares little even for the reality, and seeks refuge in an unornamented plainness. The hand-worked embroidery glorified and gave value to the material it was worked on. The machine-work cannot lift it above the commonplace. When will people understand that the more ornament is slow and difficult of production, the more we appreciate it when we have got it; that it is because we know that the thought of a human brain and the skill of a human hand went into every stroke of a chisel, every touch of a brush, or every stitch placed by the needle, that we admire, enjoy, and wonder at the statue, the picture, or the needlework that is the result of that patience and that skill; and that we do not care about the ornament at all, and that it becomes lifeless always, and often vulgar, when it has been made at little or no cost by a machine which is ready at any moment to produce any quantity more of the same thing? All ornament and pattern was once produced by hand only, therefore it was always rare and costly and was valued accordingly. Fashions did not change quickly. It was worth while to embroider a garment beautifully, for it would be worn for years, for a lifetime perhaps; and the elaborately worked counterpane would cover the bed in the guest-chamber for more than one generation.

These remarks must be understood to apply to the ordinary fancy-work and so-called "art-needlework" of the present day. Twenty years ago there would have been no ray of light in the depths to which the art of embroidery had fallen. Now for some years steady and successful efforts have been made by a few people to produce once more works worthy of the past glories of the art. They have proved to us that designers can design and that women can execute fine embroidery, but their productions are but as a drop in the ocean of inferior and valueless work.

MARY E. TURNER.

OF MATERIALS

ALMOST every fabric that is good of its kind is suitable for a ground for needlework, and any thread of silk, linen, cotton, or wool, is suitable for laying on a web, with the purpose of decorating it. Yet these materials should not be wedded indiscriminately, every surface requiring its peculiar treatment; a loose woollen fabric, for example, being best covered with wool-work rather than with silk. Not that it is necessary to work in linen thread on linen ground, in silk on silk ground, and so forth; silk upon linen, silk on canvas, wool on

Of Materials.

linen, are legitimate, because suitable combinations; it being scarcely necessary to note that linen or wool threads should not be used on silk surface, as to place the poorer on the richer material would be an error in taste. Gold thread and precious stones will of course be reserved for the richer grounds, and the more elaborate kinds of work.

A plain or a figured (damask) silk can be employed as a ground for needlework, the broken surface of a good damask sometimes enriching and helping out the design. If work is to be laid directly on silk ground, it should be rather open and light in character; if closer stitches are wanted, the principal forms are usually done on a canvas or linen backing, which is then cut out and "applied" to the final silk ground, the design being carried on and completed by lighter work of lines and curves, and by the enrichment of gold thread, and sometimes even precious stones. These two methods are a serious and dignified form of embroidery, and were often used by the great mediæval embroiderers on a rich figured or damask silk, and sometimes on plain silk, and sometimes on a silky velvet. It is not easy to procure absolutely pure "undressed" silk now, and pliable silk velvet of a suitable nature is still more difficult to obtain. Satin is, to my thinking, almost too shiny a surface for a ground, but it may, occasionally, be useful for small work. A sort of imitation called "Roman satin" is sometimes employed on account of its cheapness and effectiveness, I suppose, as it cannot be for its beauty; the texture, when much handled, being woolly and unpleasant. No one taking trouble to procure choice materials will think of making use of it.

Of Materials.

Floss silk lends itself particularly to the kind of needlework we are speaking of; there is no twist on it, the silk is pure and untouched, if properly dyed has a soft gloss, and a yielding surface that renders it quite the foremost of embroidery silks, though its delicate texture requires skilful handling. But avoid silks that profess to be floss with the difficulty in handling removed. If the old workers could use a pure untwisted floss, surely we can take the trouble to conquer this difficulty and do the same. Twisted silk, if used on a silk ground, should, I think, be rather fine; if thick and much twisted, it stands out in relief against the ground and gives a hard and ropy appearance. I am, in fact, assuming that work on so costly a material as pure thick silk is to be rather fine than coarse. Gold and silver thread is much used with silk, but it is almost impossible to keep the silver from tarnishing. Ordinary "gold passing," which consists of a gilt silver thread wound round silk, is also apt to tarnish, and should always be lacquered before using—a rather troublesome process to do at home, as the gold has to be unwound and brushed over with the lacquer, and should be dried in a warm room free from damp, or on a hot sunny day. Japanese paper-gold is useful, for the reason that it does not tarnish, though in some ways it is more troublesome to manage than the gold that can be threaded in a needle and passed through the material. It consists, like much of the ancient gold thread, of a gilded strip of paper wound round silk, the old gold being gilded vellum, when not the flat gold beaten out thin (as, by the bye, in many of the Eastern towels made to-day where the flat tinsel is very cleverly used).

Of Materials.

Of Materials.

For needlework for more ordinary uses, linen is by far the most pleasing and enduring web. Unlike silk on the one side, and wool on the other, it has scarcely any limitations in treatment, or in material suitable to be used on it. For hangings it can be chosen of a loose large texture, and covered with bold work executed in silk, linen thread, or wool, or it can be chosen of the finest thread, and covered with minute delicate stitches; it can be worked equally well in the hand, or in a frame, and usually the more it is handled the better it looks. A thick twisted silk is excellent for big and coarse work on linen, the stitches used being on the same scale, big and bold, and finer silk used sparingly if needed. White linen thread is often the material employed for linen altar cloths, coverlets, etc., and some extremely choice examples of such work are to be seen in our museums, some worked roughly with a large linen thread and big stitches, some with patient minuteness. It is hardly necessary to say how important the design of such work is.

Of Materials.

Different qualities of this material will be suggested to the embroideress by her needs; but, before passing to other things, I should not omit mention of the charming linen woven at Langdale. For some purposes it is very useful, as good linen for embroidering on is not easy to obtain. We have, however, yet to find a web which will resemble the rougher and coarser linens used for old embroideries, rather loosely woven, with a thick glossy thread, and of a heavy yet yielding substance, quite unlike the hard paper-like surfaces of machine-made linens. The Langdale linen is, of course, hand-spun and hand-made, and the flat silky thread gives a very pleasant surface; but,

Of Materials.

owing to its price and fine texture, it is not always suitable for the purposes of large hangings. Many fine examples of Persian work, such as quilts and so forth, are executed on a white cotton ground, neither very fine nor very coarse, entirely in floss silk, a variety of stitches being used, and the brightest possible colours chosen. The cool silky surface of linen, however, commends itself more to us than cotton, each country rightly choosing the materials nearest to hand, in this as in other decorative arts. Both linen and cotton are good grounds for wool-work, of which the most satisfactory kind is that done on a large scale, with a variety of close and curious stitches within bold curves and outlines.

Canvas and net are open textures of linen or cotton, and can be used either as a ground-work covered entirely with some stitch like the old-fashioned cross-stitch or tent-stitch, or some kindred mechanical stitch, or it can stand as the ground, to be decorated with bright silks. The texture of canvas being coarse, the design for it should be chosen on a large scale, and thick silk used ; floss preferably as the glossiest, but a thick twisted silk is almost equally effective, and rather easier to handle. This canvas is used frequently in seventeenth-century Italian room-hangings, either in the natural brownish colour, or dyed blue or green, the dye on it giving a dusky neutral colour which well shows up the richness of the silk.

Of woollen materials, cloth is the king; though as a ground for needle-decoration it has its limitations. It forms a good basis for appliqué, the groups of ornament being worked separately, and laid on the cloth with threads and cords of silk, gold, or wool, according to the

Of Materials.

treatment decided on. Rough serge gives a good surface for large open wool-work. Such work is quickly done, and could be made a very pleasing decoration for walls. See the delightful inventories of the worldly goods of Sir John Fastolf in the notes to the Paston Letters, where the description of green and blue worsted hangings, and "bankers" worked over with roses and boughs, and hunting scenes, make one long to emulate the rich fancies of forgotten arts, and try to plan out similar work, much of which was quite unambitious and simple, both in design and execution. "Slack," a slightly twisted wool, worsted and crewel are usually the forms of work used; of these slack wool is the pleasantest for large work, worsted being too harsh; crewel is very fine and much twisted,[1] often met

[1] Crewel, crull, curly:—

"His locks were crull as they were laid in press,"

says Chaucer of the Squire in *The Canterbury Tales*.

with in old work of a fine kind. The advantage of wool over silk in cost is obvious, and renders it suitable for the commoner uses of life, where lavishness would be out of place.

MAY MORRIS.

COLOUR

IT is not unusual to hear said of textiles and embroideries, "I like soft quiet colouring; such and such is too bright." This assertion is both right and wrong; it shows an instinctive pleasure in harmony combined with ignorance of technique. To begin with, colour cannot be too bright in itself; if it appears so, it is the skill of the craftsman that is at fault. It will be noted in a fine piece of work that far from blazing with colour in a way to disturb the eye, its general effect is that of a subdued glow; and yet, on considering the different shades of the colours used, they are found to be in themselves of the brightest the dyer can produce. Thus I have seen in an old Persian rug light and dark blue flowers and orange leaves outlined with turquoise blue on a strong red ground, a combination that sounds daring, and yet nothing could be more peaceful in tone than the beautiful and complicated groups of colours here displayed. Harmony, then, produces this repose, which is demanded instinctively, purity and crispness being further obtained by the quality of the colours used.

Thus in blues, use the shades that are only obtained satisfactorily by indigo dye, with such modifications as slightly "greening" with yellow when a green-blue is wanted, and so forth. The pure blue of indigo,[1] neither slaty nor too

[1] For notes on the dyer's art and the nature of dye stuffs, see William Morris's essay on "Dyeing as an Art," p. 196.

Colour. hot and red on the one hand, nor tending to a coarse "peacock" green-blue on the other, is perfect in all its tones, and of all colours the safest to use in masses. Its modifications to purple on one side and green-blue on the other are also useful, though to be employed with moderation. There are endless varieties of useful reds, from pink, salmon, orange, and scarlet, to blood-red and deep purple-red, obtained by different dyes and by different processes of dyeing. Kermes, an insect dye, gives a very beautiful and permanent colour, rather scarlet. Cochineal, also an insect dye, gives a red, rather inferior, but useful for mixed shades, and much used on silk, of which madder and kermes are apt to destroy the gloss, the former a good deal, the latter slightly. Madder, a vegetable dye, "yields on wool a deep-toned blood-red, somewhat bricky and tending to scarlet. On cotton and linen all imaginable shades of red, according to the process."[1] Of the shades into which red enters, avoid over-abundant use of warm orange or scarlet, which are the more valuable (especially the latter) the more sparingly used; there is a dusky orange and a faint clear bricky scarlet, sometimes met with in old work, that do not need this reservation, being quiet colours of impure yet beautiful tone. Clear, full yellow, fine in itself, also loses its value if too plentifully used, or lacking due relief by other colours. The pure colour is neither reddish and hot in tone, nor greenish and sickly It is very abundant, for example, in Persian silk embroidery, also in Chinese, and again in Spanish and Italian work of the sixteenth and seventeenth centuries. The best and most permanent yellow dye, especially

[1] William Morris, "Dyeing as an Art."

Colour. valuable on silk, is weld or "wild mignonette."

Next to blue, green seems the most natural colour to live with, and the most restful to the eye and brain; yet it is curious to those not familiar with the ins and outs of dyeing that it should be so difficult to obtain through ordinary commercial channels a full, rich, permanent green, neither muddy yellow nor coarse bluish. A dyer who employed old-fashioned dye-stuffs and methods would, however, tell us that the greens of commerce are obtained by *messes*, and not by dyes, the only method for obtaining good shades being that of dyeing a blue of the depth required in the indigo-vat, and afterwards "greening" it with yellow, with whatever modifications are needed. Three sets of greens will be found useful for needlework, full yellow-greens of two or three shades, grayish-greens, and blue-greens. Of these, the shades tending to grayish-green are the most manageable in large masses. There is also an olive-green that is good, if not too dark and brown, when it becomes a nondescript, and as such to be condemned.

Walnut (the roots or the husks or the nut) and catechu (the juice of a plant) are the most reliable brown dye-stuffs, giving good rich colour. The best black, by the bye, formerly used, consisted of the darkest indigo shade the material would take, dipped afterwards in the walnut root dye.

This hasty enumeration of dye-stuffs gives an idea of those principally used until this century, but now very rarely, since the reign of Aniline. Yet they give the only really pure and permanent colours known, not losing their value by artificial light, and very little and

Colour. gradually fading through centuries of exposure to sunlight. It would be pleasant if in purchasing silk or cloth one had not to pause and consider "will it fade?" meaning not "will it fade in a hundred, or ten, or three years?" but "will it fade and be an unsightly rag this time next month?" I cannot see that Aniline has done more for us than this.

Colour can be treated in several different ways: by distinctly light shades, whether few or many, on a dark ground, which treatment lends itself to great variety and effect; or by dark on a light ground, not so rich or satisfying in effect; or again, by colour placed on colour of equal tone, as it were a mosaic or piecing together of colours united, or "jointed," by outlining round the various members of the design. Black on white, or white on white, a mere drawing of a design on the material, scarcely comes under the head of Colour, though, as aforesaid, some very beautiful work has been done in this way.

Colour.

As regards method of colouring, it is not very possible to give much indication of what to use and what to avoid, it being greatly a matter of practice, and somewhat of instinct, how to unite colour into beautiful and complex groups. A few hints for and against certain combinations may perhaps be given: for instance, avoid placing a blue immediately against a green of nearly the same tone; an outline of a different colour disposes of this difficulty, but even so, blue and green for equally leading colours should be avoided. Again, red and yellow, if both of a vivid tone, will need a softening outline; also, I think, red and green if at all strong; avoid cold green in

Colour. contact with misty blue-green, which in itself is rather a pretty colour: the warning seems futile, but I have seen these colours used persistently together, and do not like the resulting undecided gray tone. A cold strong green renders service sometimes, notably for placing against a clear brilliant yellow, which is apt to deaden certain softer greens. Brown, when used, should be chosen carefully, warm in tint, but not *hot*; avoid the mixture of brown and yellow, often seen in "Art Depôts," but not in nature, an unfortunate groping after the picturesque, as brown wants cooling down, and to marry it to a flaming yellow is not the way to do it. Black should be used very sparingly indeed, though by no means banished from the palette. Blue and pink, blue and red, with a little tender green for relief, are perfectly safe combinations for the leading colours in a piece of work; again, yellow and green, or yellow, pink, and green, make a delightfully fresh and joyous show. There is a large coverlet to be seen at the South Kensington Museum (in the Persian gallery) which is worked in these colours, all very much the same bright tone, the centre being green and yellow and pink, and the several borders the same, with the order and proportion altered to make a variety. In recalling bright colouring like this, one is reminded of Chaucer and his unfailing delight in gay colours, which he constantly brings before us in describing garden, woodland, or beflowered gown. As—

"Everich tree well from his fellow grewe
With branches broad laden with leaves newe
That sprongen out against the sonne sheene
Some golden red and some a glad bright grene."

Colour. Or, again, the Squire's dress in the Prologue to *The Canterbury Tales*—

> "Embrouded was he, as it were a mede
> Alle ful of freshe floures, white and rede."

MAY MORRIS.

STITCHES AND MECHANISM

AS a guiding classification of methods of embroidery considered from the technical point of view, I have set down the following heads:—

(*a*) Embroidery of materials in frames.

(*b*) Embroidery of materials held in the hand.

(*c*) Positions of the needle in making stitches.

(*d*) Varieties of stitches.

(*e*) Effects of stitches in relation to materials into which they are worked.

Stitches and Mechanism.

(*f*) Methods of stitching different materials together.

(*g*) Embroidery in relief.

(*h*) Embroidery on open grounds like net, etc.

(*i*) Drawn thread work; needlepoint lace.

(*j*) Embroidery allied to tapestry weaving.

In the first place, I define embroidery as the ornamental enrichment by needle-work of a given material. Such material is usually a closely-woven stuff; but skins of animals, leather, etc., also serve as foundations for embroidery, and so do nets.

(*a*) Materials to be embroidered may be either stretched out in a frame, or held loosely (*b*) in the hand. Experience decides when either way is the better. For embroidery upon nets, frames are indispensable. The use of frames is also necessary when a particular aim of the embroiderer is to secure an even tension of stitch throughout his work. There are various frames, some large and standing on trestles ; in these many feet of material can be stretched out. Then there are small handy frames in which a square foot or two of material is stretched ; and again there are smaller frames, usually circular, in which a few inches of materials of delicate texture, like muslin and cambric, may be stretched.

Stitches and Mechanism.

Oriental embroiderers, like those of China, Japan, Persia, and India, are great users of frames for their work.

(*c*) Stitches having peculiar or individual characteristics are comparatively few. Almost all are in use for plain needlework. It is through the employment of them to render or express ornament or pattern that they become embroidery stitches. Some embroiderers and some schools of embroidery contend that the number of embroidery stitches is almost infinite. This, however, is probably one of the myths of the craft. To begin with, there are barely more than two different positions in which the needle is held for making a stitch — one when the needle is passed more or less horizontally through the material, the other when the needle is worked more or less vertically. In respect of the first-named way, the point of the needle enters the material usually in two places, and one pull takes the embroidery thread into the material more or less horizontally, or along or behind its surface (Fig. 1). In the second, the needle is passed upwards from beneath the material, pulled right through it, and then returned downwards, so that there are two pulls instead of one to complete a single stitch.

A hooked or crochet needle with a handle is held more or less vertically for working a chain stitch upon the surface of a material stretched in a frame, but

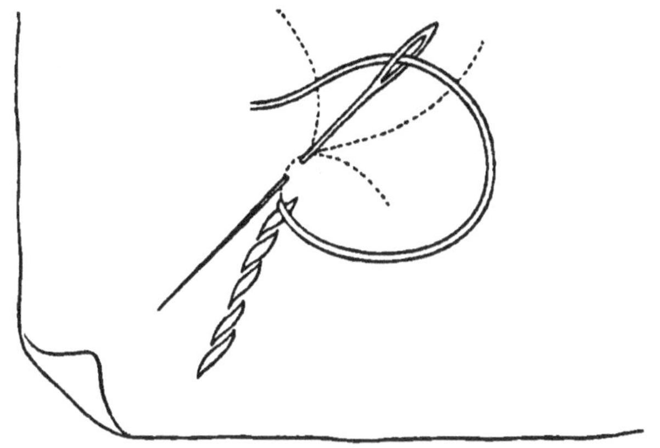

Fig. 1.—Stem Stitch—a peculiar use of short stitches.

this is a method of embroidery involving the use of an implement distinct from that done with the ordinary and freely-plied needle. Still, including this last-named method, which comes into the class of embroidery done with the needle in a more or less vertical position, we do not get more than two distinctive positions for holding the embroidery needle.

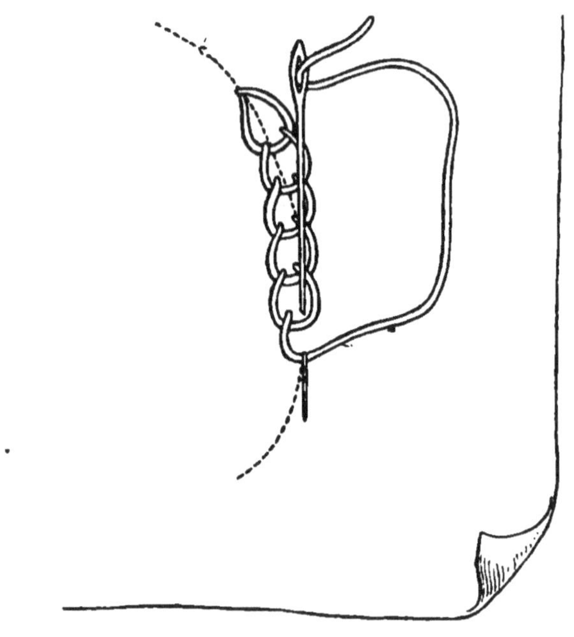

Fig. 2.—Chain Stitch.

(*d*) Varieties of stitches may be classified under two sections: one of stitches in which the thread is looped, as in chain stitch, knotted stitches, and button-hole stitch; the other of stitches in which the thread is not looped, but lies flatly, as in short and long stitches—crewel or feather stitches as they are sometimes called,—darning stitches, tent and cross stitches, and satin stitch.

Stitches and Mechanism.

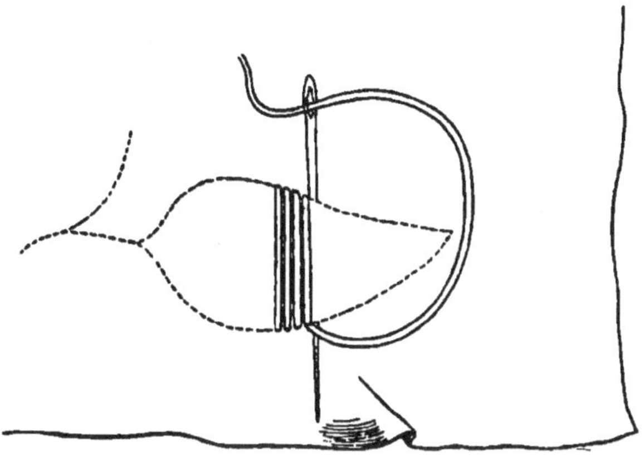

Fig. 3.—Satin Stitch.

Almost all of these stitches produce different sorts of surface or texture in the embroidery done with them. Chain stitches, for instance, give a broken or granular-looking surface (Fig. 2). This effect in surface is more strongly

Stitches and Mechanism.

marked when knotted stitches are used. Satin stitches give a flat surface (Fig. 3), and are generally used for embroidery or details which are to be of an

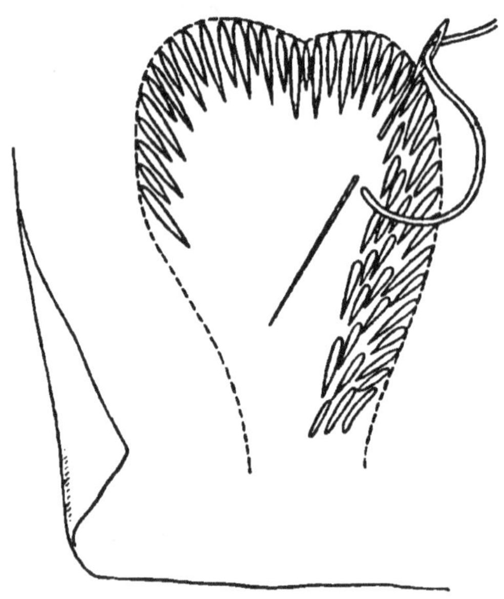

Fig. 4.—Feather or Crewel Stitch—a mixture of long and short stitches.

even tint of colour. Crewel or long and short stitches combined (Fig. 4) give a slightly less even texture than satin stitches. Crewel stitch is specially adapted to the rendering of coloured surfaces of work in which different tints are to modulate into one another.

Stitches and Mechanism.

(*e*) The effects of stitches in relation to the materials into which they are worked can be considered under two broadly-marked divisions. The one is in regard to embroidery which is to produce an effect on one side only of a material; the other to embroidery which shall produce similar effects equally on both the back and front of the material. A darning and a satin stitch may be worked so that the embroidery has almost the same effect on both sides of the material. Chain stitch and crewel stitch can only be used with regard to effect on one side of a material.

(*f*) But these suggestions for a simple classification of embroidery do not by any means apply to many methods of so-called embroidery, the effects of which depend upon something more

Stitches and Mechanism.

than stitches. In these other methods cutting materials into shapes, stitching materials together, or on to one another, and drawing certain threads out of a woven material and then working over the undrawn threads, are involved. Applied or appliqué work is generally used in connection with ornament of bold forms. The larger and principal forms are cut out of one material and then stitched down to another—the junctures of the edges of the cut-out forms being usually concealed and the shapes of the forms emphasised by cord stitched along them. Patchwork depends for successful effect upon skill in cutting out the several pieces which are to be stitched together. Patchwork is a sort of mosaic work in textile materials; and, far beyond the homely patchwork quilt of country cottages, patchwork lends itself to the production of ingenious counterchanges of form and colour in complex patterns. These methods of appliqué and patchwork are peculiarly adapted to ornamental needlework which is to lie, or hang, stretched out flatly, and are not suited therefore to work in which is involved a calculated beauty of effect from folds.

Stitches and Mechanism.

(*g*) There are two or three classes of embroidery in relief which are not well adapted to embroideries on lissome materials in which folds are to be considered. Quilting is one of these classes. It may be artistically employed for rendering low-relief ornament, by means of a stout cord or padding placed between two bits of stuff, which are then ornamentally stitched together so that the cord or padding may fill out and give slight relief to the ornamental portions defined by and enclosed between the lines of stitching. There is also padded embroidery or work consisting of a number of details separately wrought in relief over padding of hanks of thread, wadding, and such like. Effects of high

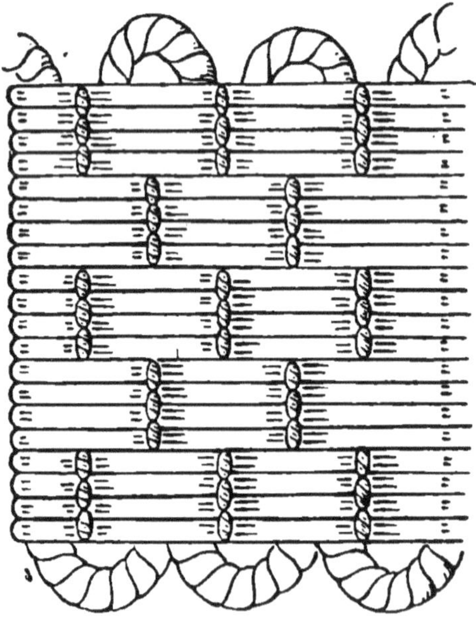

Fig. 5.—A form of Embroidery in relief, called "Couching."

relief are obtainable by this method. Another class, but of lower relief embroidery, is couching (Fig. 5), in which cords and gimps are laid side by side, in groups, upon the face of a material,

Stitches and Mechanism.

and then stitched down to it. Various effects can be obtained in this method. The colour of the thread used to stitch the cords or gimp down may be different from that of the cords or gimp, and the stitches may of course be so taken as to produce small powdered or diaper patterns over the face of the groups of cords or gimp. Gold cords are often used in this class of work, which is peculiarly identified with ecclesiastical embroideries of the fifteenth and sixteenth centuries, as also with Japanese work of later date.

(*h*) The embroidery and work hitherto alluded to has been such as requires a foundation of a closely woven nature, like linen, cloth, silk, and velvet. But there are varieties of embroidery done upon netted or meshed grounds. And on to these open grounds, embroidery in darning and chain stitches can be wrought.

Stitches and Mechanism.

For the most part the embroideries upon open or meshed grounds have a lace-like appearance. In lace, the contrast between close work and open, or partially open, spaces about it plays an important part. The methods of making lace by the needle, or by bobbins on a cushion, are totally distinct from the methods of making lace-like embroideries upon net.

(*i*) Akin to lace and embroideries upon net is embroidery in which much of its special effect is obtained by the withdrawal of threads from the material, and then either whipping or overcasting in button-hole stitches the undrawn threads. The Persians and embroiderers in the Grecian Archipelago have excelled in such work, producing wondrously delicate textile grills of ingenious geometric patterns. In this drawn thread work, as it is called, we often meet with the employment of button-hole stitching, which is an important stitch in making needlepoint lace (Fig. 6). Stitches and Mechanism.

(*j*) We also meet with the use of a weaving stitch resembling in effect, on a small scale, willow weaving for hurdles. This weaving stitch, and the method of compacting together the threads made

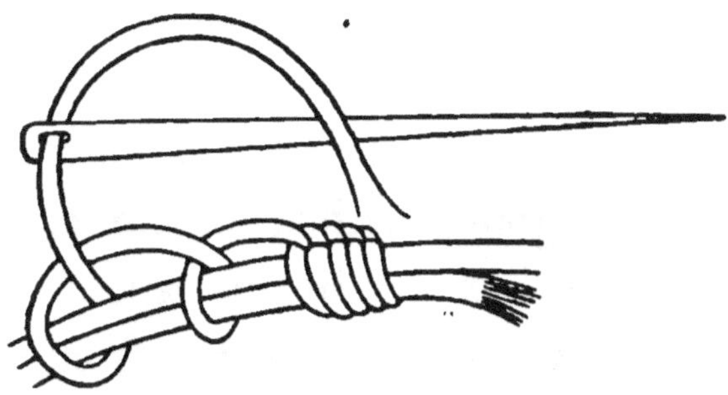

Fig. 6.—Button-hole Stitching, as used in needlepoint lace.

with it, are closely allied to that special method of weaving known as tapestry weaving. Some of the earliest specimens of tapestry weaving consist of ornamental borders, bands, and panels, which were inwoven into tunics and cloaks worn by Greeks and Romans from the fourth century before Christ, up to the eighth or ninth after Christ. The scale of the work in these is so small, as compared with that of large tapestry wall-hangings of the fifteenth century, that the method may be regarded as being related more to drawn thread embroidery than to weaving into an extensive field of warp threads.

A sketch of the different employments of the foregoing methods of embroidery is not to be included in this paper. The universality of embroidery from the earliest of historic times is attested by evidences of its practice amongst primitive tribes throughout the world. Fragments of stitched materials or undoubted indications of them have been found in the remains of early American Indians, and in the cave dwellings of men who lived thousands of years before the

Stitches and Mechanism.

period of historic Egyptians and Assyrians. Of Greek short and long stitch, and chain stitch and appliqué embroidery, there are specimens of the third or fourth century B.C. preserved in the Hermitage at St. Petersburg. Babylonians, Egyptians, Greeks, and Romans were skilful in the use of tapestry weaving stitches. Dainty embroidery, with delicate silken threads, was practised by the Chinese long before similar work was done in the countries west of Persia, or in countries which came within the Byzantine Empire. In the early days of that Empire, the Emperor Theodosius I. framed rules respecting the importation of silk, and made regulations for the labour employed in the *gynæcea*, the public weaving and embroidering rooms of that period, the development and organisation of which are traceable to the apartments allotted

Stitches and Mechanism.

in private houses to the sempstresses and embroideresses who formed part of the well-to-do households of early classic times.

ALAN S. COLE.

DESIGN

"*Drink waters out of thine own cistern, and running waters out of thine own well.*"—Solomon.

"*Produce; produce; be it but the infinitesimallest product, produce.*"—Carlyle.

FOR the last sixty years, ever since the Gothic Revival set in, we have done our best to resuscitate the art of embroidery. First the Church and then the world took up the task, and much admirable work has been done by the "Schools," the shops, and at home. And yet the verdict still must be "the old is better."

Considering all things, this lack of absolute success is perplexing and needs

Design. to be explained. For we have realised our ideals. Never was a time when the art and science of needlework were so thoroughly understood as in England at the present moment. Our designers can design in any style. Every old method is at our fingers' ends. Every ingenious stitch of old humanity has been mastered, and a descriptive name given to it of our own devising. Every traditional pattern—wave, lotus, daisy, convolvulus, honeysuckle, "Sacred Hom" or tree of life; every animal form, or bird, fish or reptile, has been traced to its source, and its symbolism laid bare. Every phase of the world's primal schools of design—Egyptian, Babylonian, Indian, Chinese, Greek, Byzantine, European—has been illustrated and made easy of imitation. We are archæologists: we are critics: we are artists. We are lovers of old work: we are learned in historical and æsthetic questions, in technical rules and principles of design. We are colourists, and can play with colour as musicians play with notes. What is more, we are in terrible earnestness about the whole business. The honour of the British nation, the credit of Royalty, are, in a manner, staked upon the success of our "Schools of Needlework." And yet, in spite of all these favouring circumstances, we get no nearer to the old work that first mocked us to emulation in regard to power of initiative and human interest.

Truth and gallantry prompt me to add, it is not in stitchery but in design that we lag behind the old. Fair English hands can copy every trick of ancient artistry: finger-skill was never defter, will was never more ardent to do fine things, than now. Yet our work hangs fire. It fails in design. Why?

Design.

Now, Emerson has well said that all the arts have their origin in some enthusiasm. Mark this, however: that whereas the design of old needlework is based upon enthusiasm for birds, flowers, and animal life,[1] the design of modern needlework has its origin in enthusiasm for antique art. Nature is, of course, the groundwork of all art, even of ours; but it is not to Nature at first-hand that we go. The flowers we embroider were not plucked from field and garden, but from the camphor-scented preserves at Kensington. Our needlework conveys no pretty message of

"The life that breathes, the life that lives,"

it savours only of the now stiff and stark device of dead hands. Our art holds no mirror up to Nature as we

[1] A strip of sixteenth-century needlework in my possession (6 ft. by 2 ft. 6 in.) figures thirty different specimens of plants, six animals, and four birds, besides ornamental sprays of foliage.

see her, it only reflects the reflection of dead periods. Nay, not content with merely rifling the *motifs* of moth-fretted rags, we must needs turn for novelty to an old Persian tile which, well magnified, makes a capital design for a quilt that one might perchance sleep under in spite of what is outside! Or we are not ashamed to ask our best embroideresses to copy the barbaric wriggles and child-like crudities of a seventh-century "Book of Kells," a task which cramps her style and robs Celtic art of all its wonder.

We have, I said, realised our ideals. We can do splendidly what we set ourselves to do—namely, to mimic old masterpieces. The question is, What next? Shall we continue to hunt old trails, and die, not leaving the world richer than we found it? Or shall we for art and honour's sake boldly adventure something—drop this wearisome

Design. translation of old styles and translate Nature instead?

Think of the gain to the "Schools," and to the designers themselves, if we elect to take another starting-point! No more museum-inspired work! No more scruples about styles! No more dry-as-dust stock patterns! No more loathly Persian-tile quilts! No more awful "Zoomorphic" table-cloths! No more cast-iron-looking altar cloths, or Syon Cope angels, or stumpy Norfolk-screen saints! No more Tudor roses and pumped-out Christian imagery suggesting that Christianity is dead and buried! But, instead, we shall have design *by* living men *for* living men—something that expresses fresh realisations of sacred facts, personal broodings, skill, joy in Nature—in grace of form and gladness of colour; design that shall recall Shakespeare's maid who

“ . . . with her neeld composes
Nature’s own shape, of bud, bird, branch, or berry,
That even Art sisters the natural roses.”

For, after all, modern design should be as the old—living thought, artfully expressed : fancy that has taken fair shapes. And needlework is still a pictorial art that requires a real artist to direct the design, a real artist to ply the needle. Given these, and our needlework can be as full of story as the Bayeux tapestry, as full of imagery as the Syon Cope, and better drawn. The charm of old embroidery lies in this, that it clothes current thought in current shapes. It meant something to the workers, and to the man in the street for whom it was done. And for our work to gain the same sensibility, the same range of appeal, the same human interest, we must employ the same means. We must clothe modern ideas

Design. in modern dress; adorn our design with living fancy, and rise to the height of our knowledge and capacities.

Doubtless there is danger to the untrained designer in direct resort to Nature. For the tendency in his or her case is to copy outright, to give us pure crude fact and not to *design* at all. Still there is hope in honest error: none in the icy perfections of the mere stylist. For the unskilled designer there is no training like drawing from an old herbal; for in all old drawing of Nature there is a large element of design. Besides which, the very limitations of the materials used in realising a design in needlework, be it ever so naturally coloured, hinders a too definite presentation of the real.

For the professional stylist, the confirmed conventionalist, an hour in his garden, a stroll in the embroidered meadows, a dip into an old herbal, a few carefully-drawn cribs from Curtis's *Botanical Magazine*, or even — for lack of something better — Sutton's last Illustrated Catalogue, is wholesome exercise, and will do more to revive the original instincts of a true designer than a month of sixpenny days at a stuffy museum. The old masters are dead, but "the flowers," as Victor Hugo says, "the flowers last always."

JOHN D. SEDDING.

ON DESIGNING FOR THE ART OF EMBROIDERY

IN every form of art the thing which is of primary importance is the question of Design.

By Design I understand the inventive arrangement of lines and masses, for their own sake, in such a relation to one another, that they form a fine, harmonious whole : a whole, that is, towards which each part contributes, and is in such a combination with every other part that the result is a unity of effect, so completely satisfying us that we have no sense of demanding in it more or less.

After this statement and definition let me proceed to touch briefly upon four points in relation to the matter, as it concerns itself with the art of Embroidery; and the first of these four points shall be this. Before you commence your design, consider carefully the conditions under which the finished work is to be seen. There is a tendency in embroidery to be too uniformly delicate and minute. To be too delicate, or even minute, in something which is always to be seen close under one's eyes is, it may be, impossible; but in an altar-cloth, a banner, a wall-hanging, this delicacy and minuteness are not merely thrown away, but they tend to make the thing ineffective. For such objects as these I have mentioned, the main lines and masses of the design should, it would seem in the nature of the case, be well emphasised; if they are

On Designing for the Art of Embroidery.

well emphasised, and of course fine in their character and arrangement, there is produced a sense of largeness and dignity which is of the highest value, and for the absence of which no amount of curious workmanship will atone. In making your design, let these main lines and masses be the first things you attend to, and secure. Stand away at a distance, and see if they tell out satisfactorily, before you go on to put in a single touch of detail.

For the second point: remember that embroidery deals with its objects as if they were all on the same plane. It has been sometimes described as the art of painting with the needle; but it necessarily and essentially differs from the art of painting in this, that it, properly, represents all things as being equally near to you, as laid out before you on the same plane. It would seem, therefore, to be a sound rule to fill the spaces, left for you by the arrangement of your main lines and masses, with such forms as shall occupy these spaces, one by one, completely; with such patterns, I mean, as shall appear to have their natural and full development within the limits of each space: avoid the appearance of one thing being behind the other, with portions of it cut off and obscured by what comes in front of it. But in this, as in so much else, an immense deal must be left to the instinct of the artist.

Thirdly: aim at simplicity in the elements or motives of your design; do not crowd it with a score of different elements, which produce a sense of confusion and irritation, and, in reality, prove only a poverty of invention. A real richness of invention, as well as a richness of effect, lies in using one or two, perhaps at most three, elements, with variety in the treatment of them. Make yourself thoroughly master of the essential points, in whatever elements you choose as the basis of your design, before you set pencil to paper ; and you will find in almost any natural form you fix upon more than enough to give you all the variety and richness you require, if you have sufficient natural fancy to play with it.

Lastly : return again and again, and for evermore, to Nature. The value of studying specimens of old embroidery is immense ; it makes you familiar with the principles and methods, which experience has found to be true and useful ; it puts you into possession of the traditions of the art. He that has no reverence for the traditions of his art seals his own doom ; he that is careless about them, or treats them with superciliousness, or will not give the time and pains necessary to understand them, but thinks to start off afresh along clean new lines of his own, stamps himself as an upstart—makes himself perhaps, if he is clever, a nine days' curiosity—but loses himself, by and by, in extravagances, and brings no fruit to perfection. The study of old work, then, is of the highest importance, is essential; the patient and humble study of it. But for what end? To learn principles and methods, to secure a sound foundation for oneself; not to slavishly imitate results, and live on bound hand and foot in the swaddling clothes of precedent. Learn your business in the schools, but go out to Nature for your inspirations. See Nature through your own eyes, and be a persistent and curious observer of her infinite wonders. Yet to see Nature in herself is not everything, it is but half

On Designing for the Art of Embroidery.

the matter; the other half is to know how to use her for the purposes of fine art, to know how to translate her into the language of art. And this knowledge we acquire by a sound acquaintance with the essential conditions of whatever art we practise, a frank acceptance of these conditions, and a reverential appreciation of the teaching and examples of past workmen. Timidity and impudence are both alike fatal to an artist: timidity, which makes it impossible for him to see with his own eyes, and find his own methods; and impudence, which makes him imagine that his own eyes, and his own methods, are the best that ever were.

SELWYN IMAGE.

Printed by R. & R. CLARK, *Edinburgh*

FROM THE

Recent Publications

OF

MESSRS. PERCIVAL

KING STREET, COVENT GARDEN
LONDON

34 King Street, Covent Garden,
London, W.C.

April 1893.

Crown 8vo. With Illustrations. 6*s.*

Recollections of Dr. John Brown

Author of 'Rab and His Friends.'

With Selections from Correspondence.

By ALEXANDER PEDDIE, M.D., F.R.C.P.E., F.R.S.E., Etc.

Demy 16*mo.* 3*s.*

My Book of Songs and Sonnets

By MAUDE EGERTON KING.

Crown 8vo. 6*s.*

Outlines of British Colonisation

By the Rev. WILLIAM PARR GRESWELL, M.A.

Author of 'Our South African Empire,' 'A History of the Dominion of Canada,' and 'Geography of Africa South of the Zambesi,' etc.

With an Introduction by LORD BRASSEY.

Contents.—The West Indies—The Leeward Islands—Newfoundland—The Dominion of Canada—The West African Settlements—The South African Colonies—The Australian Colonies—Tasmania—South Australia—New Zealand—The Islands of the Pacific and Fiji—Ceylon and the Maldive Archipelago—Mauritius—Hong Kong—Appendices of Facts and Figures.

Crown 8vo. 6s.

From Advent to Advent

Sermons preached at the Chapel Royal, Whitehall.

By the late AUBREY L. MOORE, M.A.

Third Edition. Crown 8vo. 3s. 6d.

Some Aspects of Sin

Three Courses of Sermons.

By the late AUBREY L. MOORE, M.A.

Crown 8vo. 3s. 6d.

The Message of the Gospel

Addresses to Candidates for Ordination, and Sermons preached chiefly before the University of Oxford.

By the late AUBREY L. MOORE, M.A.

Crown 8vo. 7s. 6d.

The Fire upon the Altar

Sermons preached to Harrow Boys. 1887 to 1890.

By the Rev. J. E. C. WELLDON, M.A.,
Head Master of Harrow School, and Hon. Chaplain to the Queen.

Crown 8vo. 7s. 6d.

Old Truths in Modern Lights

The Boyle Lectures for 1890, with other Sermons.

By T. G. BONNEY, D.Sc., LL.D., F.R.S., F.S.A., F.G.S.,
Fellow of St. John's College, Cambridge, Honorary Canon of Manchester.

London: 34 King Street, Covent Garden.

Second Edition. Demy 8vo. 2s. 6d.

High and Low Church

By LORD NORTON.

Being a Discussion relating to Differences of Views within the Church of England as to matters connected with its Doctrine and Practice.

Crown 8vo. 5s.

Things Old and New

Sermons and Papers.

By the Rev. G. H. FOWLER,
Late Principal of the Clergy School, Leeds.

With a Preface by the Rev. Dr. TALBOT, Vicar of Leeds.

Crown 8vo. With Illustrations. 1s.

Plain Handicrafts

Being Essays by Artists setting forth the Principles of Design and Established Methods of Workmanship.

A Guide to Elementary Practice.

Edited by A. H. MACKMURDO.

With a Preface by G. F. WATTS, R.A.

Eleventh Thousand. Fcap 8vo. 1s. 6d.

Popular Lessons on Cookery

By Mrs. BOYD CARPENTER.

Post Free to Subscribers, Ten Shillings a year, paid in advance; or Three Shillings a Number.

The Economic Review

A Quarterly Review for the Consideration of Social and Economic Questions.

In Connection with the Oxford University Branch of the Christian Social Union.

CONTENTS OF THE APRIL NUMBER, 1893.

The History of English Serfdom. Prof. W. J. ASHLEY, M.A.
Edward Vansittart Neale as Christian Socialist. His Honour JUDGE HUGHES, Q.C.
The Ethics of Wills. The Rev. T. C. FRY, D.D.
Co-operators and Profit-Sharing. W. E. SNELL.
The Alcohol Monopoly in Switzerland. JOSEPH KING.
The Special Importance of the study of Christian Ethics for the Church in the present day. The Rev. R. L. OTTLEY, M.A.
Legislation, Parliamentary Inquiries, and Official Returns. EDWIN CANNAN, M.A.
Reviews and Short Notices.

Crown 8vo. 6*s.*

The Religion of Humanity

And other Poems.

By ANNIE MATHESON.

Folio. 1*s.*

Technical Exercises for the Pianoforte

By BASIL JOHNSON,
Organist of Rugby School.

Second Edition, Revised. In two Volumes. Crown 8vo. 16*s.*

With numerous Illustrations,
including Pen and Pencil Drawings by JANE E. COOK.

Also a large-paper edition *de luxe* of *Thirty-six* signed and numbered copies, with the illustrations hand printed upon Japanese paper and mounted, price Five Guineas net each.

Old Touraine

The Life and History of the Famous Châteaux of France.

By THEODORE ANDREA COOK, B.A.,
sometime Scholar of Wadham College, Oxford.

There is an itinerary for the tourist, and a map, genealogical tables, lists of pictures, manuscripts, etc., and an index, which will, it is hoped, save the necessity of purchasing guide-books for each of the Châteaux.

In two Volumes. Large Post 8vo. 21*s. net.*

A Paradise of English Poetry

Arranged by the REV. H. C. BEECHING, M.A.,
Rector of Yattendon, Berks.

This work is printed on hand-made paper, bound in buckram, and published in a limited edition, which will not, under any circumstances, be reprinted. The publishers reserve the right to issue at a future date, should they think fit, a smaller and cheaper edition.

'That those who walk in the rose-scented avenues of Mr. Beeching's garden will say that the planting has been well done, we cannot doubt for a moment. He has not only a knowledge of English literature which is as sympathetic as it is profound, but he has the critical faculty, without which a knowledge of, and even a love for, literature is wasted. He does more than know what is good in litera ture,—that is comparatively easy. He knows what is bad, and with him base metal is never offered us for gold. There are not many men who can stand this test, but Mr. Beeching comes through it triumphantly. . . . Before we leave this book, we must commend Mr. Beeching's excellent notes. They are interesting, to the point, not too long, and often enable one to get an additional touch of pleasure from the verse they annotate.'—**Spectator.**

A very skilful selection, and eminently worthy of its name. . . . Will commend itself to all true lovers of English poetry.' —**Times.**

Crown 8vo. 7*s.* 6*d.*

The Art Teaching of John Ruskin

By W. G. COLLINGWOOD, M.A.

Crown 8vo. With Illustrations. 5*s.*

The Dawn of Art in the Ancient World

An Archæological Sketch.

By WILLIAM MARTIN CONWAY.

Sometime Roscoe Professor of Art in University College, Liverpool, Victoria University.

Crown 8vo. 7*s.* 6*d.*

With Frontispiece and Thirty Illustrations in the Text.

Architecture, Mysticism, and Myth

An Essay in Comparative Architecture, being an Inquiry as to the Basis of certain Ideas common to the Sacred Buildings of many Lands.

By W. R. LETHABY.

Royal 16mo. 5*s.*

Love's Looking-Glass

A Volume of Poems.

By the Authors of 'Love in Idleness.'

'A little volume of poems entitled "Love in Idleness," was published a few years ago by three Oxford friends—Mr. J. W. Mackail, Mr. H. C. Beeching, and Mr. J. B. B. Nichols—and being speedily appreciated by all lovers of graceful and scholarly versification, it soon went out of print. The three writers now reappear in the same association in "Love's Looking-Glass," which contains the original poems, together with many additions. . . . The volume should prove as attractive as its predecessor, for the new poems it contains are not less scholarly, melodious, and graceful than the old.'—**Times.**

'This delightful volume of verse. . . . All the verse is full of an academic spirit, but it is that spirit in its happiest mood, without a touch of pedantry or artificiality.'—**Spectator.**

Demy 16mo. 3s. 6d. each.
Bound in paper boards, with parchment back.

The Pocket Library of English Literature

Edited by GEORGE SAINTSBURY.

VOL. I.—TALES OF MYSTERY.
VOL. II.—POLITICAL VERSE.
VOL. III.—DEFOE'S MINOR NOVELS.
VOL. IV.—POLITICAL PAMPHLETS.

'Mr. George Saintsbury is the editor, and, as nobody living has a purer, wider, or better instructed taste than his in English literature, the series promises good things to a lover of books. Mr. Saintsbury's introduction to the extracts (Tales of Mystery) is an interesting sketch in criticism, and enables a reader to see at once what is best in the stories themselves.' —**Scotsman.**

'It is not surprising to find that this volume ("Seventeenth Century Lyrics") wherein are gathered so many lyric gems, has passed into a second edition. . . . It is almost unnecessary to say that Mr. Saintsbury's selections are admirable, and there are few poems excluded which we could wish admitted, fewer still admitted which we should desire excluded.'—**Birmingham Daily Gazette.**

VOL. V.—SEVENTEENTH CENTURY LYRICS. *Second Edition.*
VOL. VI.—ELIZABETHAN AND JACOBEAN PAMPHLETS

'Mr. Saintsbury's selections from all three writers are fairly representative; indeed, those from Mrs. Radcliffe and Maturin show a nicety of judgment which the most fastidious critic cannot but approve.'—**Saturday Review.**

'We cannot part with the charming chaplets (Political Verse) which Mr. Saintsbury has arranged, without thanking him for the result of his wide knowledge, his untiring industry, and his impartial comprehensiveness of view.'—**Daily News.**

'"Political Verse." A most readable and entertaining volume.'—**Times.**

'"Political Pamphlets" is a very attractive volume.'—**Times.**

'We are heartily glad that Mr. Saintsbury has put together his pretty little volumes.'—**Spectator.**

The 'Seventeenth Century Lyrics' may also be had bound in Cloth, gilt lettered, 3s. 6d.

Second Edition, Revised. Crown 8vo. 7s. 6d.

Essays in English Literature

1780 to 1860.

By GEORGE SAINTSBURY.

CONTENTS.—The kinds of Criticism — Crabbe — Hogg (Ettrick Shepherd)—Sydney Smith—Jeffrey—Hazlitt—Moore—Leigh Hunt—Peacock—Wilson (Christopher North)—De Quincey—Lockhart—Praed—Borrow.

Second Edition, Revised. Crown 8vo. 7s. 6d.

Essays on French Novelists

By GEORGE SAINTSBURY.

CONTENTS.—The Present State of the French Novel—Anthony Hamilton—Alain René Lesage—A Study of Sensibility—Charles de Bernard—Alexandre Dumas—Théophile Gautier—Jules Sandeau—Octave Feuillet—Gustave Flaubert—Henry Murger—Victor Cherbuliez.

As a judge of romantic literature Mr. Saintsbury stands on a very high eminence indeed, and few will deny that a critic of his taste and penetration is well qualified to act as *cicerone* to excursionists into those fields of fiction.'—**Times.**

'We should like to notice many masterly touches of critical knowledge and insight, many delightful remarks which no worthy reader will pass over or forget, but this is really not necessary. Everybody who knows Mr. Saintsbury's former books will read and enjoy this book. There are few studies more fascinating than that of French literature.'—**Spectator.**

Crown 8vo. 7s. 6d.

Miscellaneous Essays

By GEORGE SAINTSBURY.

CONTENTS.—English Prose Style—Chamfort and Rivarol—Modern English Prose (1876)—Ernest Renan—Thoughts on Republics—Saint-Evremond—Charles Baudelaire—The Young England Movement; its place in our History—A Paradox on Quinet—The Contrasts of English and French Literature—A Frame of Miniatures:—Parny, Dorat, Désaugiers, Vadé, Piron, Panard—The Present State of the English Novel (1892).

Crown 8vo. 6s.

A Guide to Greek Tragedy

For English Readers.

By the Rev. L. CAMPBELL, LL.D.,

Emeritus Professor of Greek in the University of St. Andrews.

Crown 8vo. 7s. 6d.

Studies in Secondary Education

Edited by ARTHUR H. D. ACLAND, M.P.,
Vice-President of the Council of Education;
and
H. LLEWELLYN SMITH, M.A, B.Sc.,

With an Introduction by the Right Hon. JAMES BRYCE, M.P.,
Chancellor of the Duchy of Lancaster.

Published under the Auspices of the National Association for the promotion of Technical and Secondary Education.

Crown 8vo. 5s.

Teachers' Guild Addresses, and the Registration of Teachers

By S. S. LAURIE, LL.D.
Professor of the Theory, History, and Art of Education in the University of Edinburgh.

CONTENTS.—The Philosophy of Mind, and the Training of Teachers—Theory, and the Curriculum of Secondary Schools—Method, and the Sunday School Teacher—Montaigne, the Rationalist—Roger Ascham, the Humanist—Comenius, the Encyclopædist and Founder of Method—The Schoolmaster and University (Day) Training Colleges—Selection from Evidence given before a Select Parliamentary Committee on a Teachers' Registration and Organisation Bill—Report of Select Committee of the House of Commons.

Crown 8vo. 7s. 6d.

Thirteen Essays on Education

Edited by the Hon. and Rev. E. LYTTELTON, M.A.,
Head Master of Haileybury College.

MESSRS. PERCIVAL *issue the undermentioned Catalogues, which may be had on application:—*

Crown 8vo.

1. A SELECTION FROM THEIR RECENT PUBLICATIONS IN GENERAL LITERATURE.

Crown 8vo.

2. A CATALOGUE OF EDUCATIONAL WORKS.

Demy 8vo.

3. COMPLETE CATALOGUE OF ALL THEIR PUBLICATIONS,

www.ingramcontent.com/pod-product-compliance
Lightning Source LLC
Chambersburg PA
CBHW031822270326
41932CB00008B/517

* 9 7 8 3 3 3 7 3 6 7 4 7 3 *